W. Diette

An exciting book
& on Koinonia

This bk. would be int. to report on to
a staff, study group, etc.

Pauline Partnership
in Christ

Pauline Partnership in Christ

*Christian Community and Commitment
in Light of Roman Law*

J. PAUL SAMPLEY

FORTRESS PRESS   Philadelphia

COPYRIGHT © 1980 BY FORTRESS PRESS

Library of Congress Cataloging in Publication Data

Sampley, J   Paul.
    Pauline partnership in Christ.

    Bibliography: p.
    Includes index.
    1.   Church—Biblical teaching.   2.   Mission of the church—Biblical teaching.   3.   Christian life—Biblical teaching.   4.   Partnership (Roman law).
    5.   Bible.   N.T.   Epistles of Paul—Theology.
    I.   Title.
    BS2655.C5S25   262   79-8895
    ISBN 0-8006-0631-0

8016L80   Printed in the United States of America   1-631

For my parents

Roy C. Sampley, Sr.
Mary Downs Sampley

and

Joseph C. Backus, Sr.
Myrtle Wortham Backus (†1975)

Contents

Preface

Paul was "entrusted with a commission" (1 Cor. 9:17) to preach the gospel to the Gentiles. "For the sake of the gospel" (9:23) he freely adapted himself and his preaching to his differing audiences. Paul's relations with his diverse Christian congregations were varied; so were his ways of conceptualizing how Christians related to one another and lived out their obligations and commitments to one another. But no matter how much he might have flexed this way or that, his goal in preaching remained the same: "that I might win the more" (9:19). "I have become all things to all men, that I might by all means save some" (9:22).

Recent studies of the early church, and indeed of Paul's letters, have shown that not only did the church stand over against the culture in some definite ways, but it also reflected the social world in which it found itself. The Greco-Roman culture, in which Paul and his converts lived, offered a plethora of organizations, associations, and ways of making commitments. The secular world offered the raw materials of community and commitment out of which Paul creatively fashioned his understanding of the way Christians should live together and comprehend their obligations to one another and to the world. When Paul received the gospel and recognized it as the power of God for salvation to those who believed, he did not receive with it a pristine set of categories by which the new life could be conceptualized. Refracted in the light of the gospel, the culture's associations and senses of obligation were transformed by Paul so that Christians could understand their new situation in Christ.

The following study sheds light on one hitherto unnoticed

Pauline adaptation of an association model/prevalent in his own time, a common and convenient partnership whereby individuals bind together in pursuit of a shared interest or goal. The partnership of consensual *societas* is a commonplace in Roman law. As Paul sees it the partnership is "in Christ" and requires that the believers live with one another according to the standards of the gospel and preach that gospel to those outside the faith. This partnership in Christ stands alongside other, better-known models of Christian community in the Pauline proclamation, and flowers where the requisite conditions of parity, good faith, and mutual trust are present.

Though this study has as its primary aim the identification and analysis of Paul's use of the *societas* partnership as a model of Christian community, it also sheds light on other themes and topics that have drawn considerable scholarly attention. Among these other issues are Christian freedom, the imitation of Paul, the collection for the saints in Jerusalem, Paul's support of his preaching mission, and his claims about Titus and Timothy, his fellow workers.

Inevitably a work such as this places one in heavy indebtedness to those who have assisted and supported the research. Among these must be named Indiana University for the sabbatical leave in which the study of Roman rhetorical and legal traditions was begun. The research could not have continued without the libraries at Smith College and Yale University and their cooperative staffs.

My especial appreciation goes to Wayne A. Meeks for his careful critique of this book in one of its earlier forms. He must be granted total immunity, however, from responsibility for any of its flaws.

Staretta Reynolds Kelley has my gratitude for her patience and care in deciphering my nearly illegible handwriting and in typing the manuscript.

Thanks to Sally, my partner in and for life.

Abbreviations

AAASH	*Acta Antiqua Academiae Scientiarum Hungaricae*
AJP	*American Journal of Philology*
BHTh	*Beiträge zur historischen Theologie*
Bib	*Biblica*
BullCSR	*Bulletin of the Council on the Study of Religion* .
CLJ	*Cambridge Law Journal*
CH	*Church History*
EHR	*Economic History Review*
ExpT	*The Expository Times*
ILR	*Israel Law Review*
JBL	*Journal of Biblical Literature*
LLJ	*Law Library Journal*
MLR	*Missouri Law Review*
NTS	*New Testament Studies*
NT	*Novum Testamentum*
QI	*La Question d'Israel*
RAC	*Reallexikon für Antike und Christentum*
RechScRel	*Recherches de Science religieuse*
RSR	*Religious Studies Review*
RIDA	*Revue International des droits de l'antiquité*
TDNT	*Theological Dictionary of the New Testament*
ZNW	*Zeitschrift für die neutestamentliche Wissenschaft*
ZTK	*Zeitschrift für Theologie und Kirche*

1

"Atmosphere of the Age": The Context and Purpose of This Study

At the beginning of this century W. E. B. Ball wrote:

> St. Paul is perhaps of all writers, either ancient or modern, the most difficult to understand. It cannot be that his obscurity is deliberate. It is due chiefly, no doubt, to our ignorance of the intellectual atmosphere of the age in which he lived. It is not suggested that a study of the Roman law as it existed in the first century will afford an explanation of all the perplexing passages in which the Pauline Epistles abound, but it is certain that no satisfactory commentary upon these Epistles will ever be produced except by an author who, in addition to other qualifications, is a thorough master of the history of civil jurisprudence.[1]

Ball echoes the ancient assessment of Paul—"There are some things in them [Paul's letters] hard to understand" (2 Pet. 3:16) —but he places the responsibility for dealing with the difficulties on Paul's interpreters and urges a greater knowledge of the social and legal context in which Paul preached and wrote. Recent scholarship is enlarging our view of the social world of early Christianity;[2] more particularly, several persons are scrutinizing the influence of Roman jurisprudence[3] upon Paul's correspondence.

Fascination with Paul's judicial knowledge reaches back almost to the time of the apostle. Luke, the author of the Acts of the Apostles, was the first interpreter to focus on the possibilities of Paul's Roman citizenship and his knowledge of his rights under the law.[4] Since Luke various interpreters from Augustine to the present have even deemed Paul learned in jurisprudence.[5]

In modern times, especially since the turn of this century, a range of studies has observed the impact of legal matters on the Pauline correspondence. Investigations into slavery and its connection with the Pauline letters were prompted by curiosity concerning Onesimus, the runaway slave mentioned in the Letter to Philemon, by the addresses to the slaves concerning their comportment in the household (1 Cor. 7:21–23; cf. Eph. 6:5 and Col. 3:22 ff.), and by Paul's metaphorical use of *slave* to describe his dependence on Jesus Christ as his Lord (Rom. 1:1; Gal. 1:10; Phil. 1:1; cf. Rom. 6:15–23).[6]

Likewise *redemption (apolytrōsis)* in the Pauline letters (Rom. 3:24; 8:23; 1 Cor. 1:30) has been identified as a technical term of slavery law in the Greco-Roman world.[7] Aphorisms such as "you were bought with a price" (1 Cor. 6:20 and 7:23) derive from the same social context.

In issues touching on family life Roman legal traditions and practice provided some of the everyday categories that Paul stitched into the fabric of his communications. Paul's indebtedness to legal traditions in his advice concerning divorce (1 Cor. 7:10–16)[8] and in his use of "adoption" as a theological category (Rom. 8:12–17 and Gal. 4:4–7)[9] have been studied. Also the terminology of inheritance and wills (Gal. 4:7; Rom. 8:17)[10] has been examined against the background provided by Roman jurisprudence.

During the last two decades, investigations of Roman legal traditions in the Pauline correspondence have shown renewed vigor. In some respects, contemporary studies represent a reworking of positions established in the earlier part of this century. The results of the contemporary research may be different from those reached in the early 1900s, but many of the questions have remained essentially the same. What is Paul's view of adoption and where did he get it? How do Roman laws concerning adoption help us understand Romans 8 and Galatians 4?[11] Or what is Paul's view of slavery as an institution, and what informed that perspective?[12]

Most recently, however, not only are the old issues being reexamined, but new questions are being asked about the relation of Paul's letters with Roman legal traditions. For example, one investigator has argued that Paul's use of the term *pistis*, "faith," as found in the particular formula *pistis christou* in Galatians, owes something to one Roman means of dealing with inheritance.[13] Seeing the use of commercial and legal terms in the opening chapters of Romans, another interpreter has declared that Paul cast his gospel in contract terminology, depicting the Christians as "under contract" to live in a certain way.[14]

Although researchers have established a pervasive and considerable presence of legal conceptions in Paul's preaching of the gospel, one might raise a question concerning the relation of this use of legal categories to Paul's condemnation of the Corinthians for going to court with one another (1 Cor. 6). It was a commonplace of the times, an ingredient of what Ball calls the atmosphere of the age, that civil courts were not to be trusted for justice. Even Roman citizens did not have equal opportunity before the law.[15] Wealth, position, and standing—in the Roman world the three were inseparable—were the best assurance of favorable judgment in the courts.[16] Social status and legal privilege went hand in hand. Not only did most Roman citizens shun the civil courts; so also did the Jews.[17] Whether motivated by exclusivism or some other, more practical evaluation of limited prospects for favorable judgment, the Jews of the Roman empire generally avoided the civil courts.[18]

Paul understood that the Corinthian Christians were taking their disagreements before the civil courts (1 Cor. 6:1 ff.). From Paul's vantage point it was a shameful matter (6:5). Paul and most other people in the Roman world advise against turning to the civil courts, but Paul's reason is distinctive. Though we must grant that Paul has no respect for the officials, the magistrates— they are "unbelievers" (6:6) and are properly held in no esteem

3

by the church (6:4)—his advice is not based on a skeptical reckoning of the statistical probability of justice being rendered in the civil courts. Not at all. Rather, from Paul's view, the Corinthian Christians should avoid the courts because of what has happened in Christ. Do they not know that the saints are to judge the world, yes, even angels? And if they are supposed to be competent to judge the world and even angels, how much more matters relating to this life (1 Cor. 6:2-3). Paul finds their conduct shameful because the Christians have gone to the world to have justice and righteousness defined for them.[19]

The key to Paul's position is found in his eschatological vision. By virtue of their being "washed," "sanctified," and "justified in the name of the Lord Jesus Christ and in the Spirit of our God" (6:11), the Christians will "judge the world" (6:2). The Corinthians, by their court actions against one another, show shameful ignorance not only of their status in Christ but also of their proper relation to the world. As Conzelmann has put it: "The apocalyptic idea of the role of the 'saints' in the last judgment is reinterpreted in terms of the present . . . in the sense that the church . . . practices its eschatological sovereignty in the world. . . . Paul can maintain the eschatological interpretation, because for him eschatology leads not to the negation of the present but to a critique of it. . . . The forms of the world's life are subjected to eschatological neutralization and can therefore be taken over."[20]

What does Paul suggest the Corinthians do? Escape from the world in some way? Hardly. The Corinthians had apparently misunderstood an earlier letter from Paul in which he had urged them "not to associate with immoral men" (5:9). They had taken that admonition to refer to all persons outside the church, whereas Paul had intended it of "any one who bears the name of brother" (5:11). Paul follows their interpretation of his earlier correspondence to its logical consequences and, with what is probably one of Paul's closest approximations to humor, says if they were to avoid all immoral men "you would need to go out

4

of the world" (5:10). No, the Christians are to stay in the world, to live where they are called (1 Cor. 7:20–21 and 7:29–31). Just as Paul does not counsel the Corinthians to flee the world, so also he has no program for the reform or overthrow of the civil courts.[21]

Instead he calls for the Christians to exercise their full freedom in the world and to settle their own disputes within the Christian community. "Can it be that there is not a single wise man [*sophos*] among you able to give a decision?" (6:5, NEB). With considerable irony Paul asks how it is possible that the Corinthians, who vaunt themselves on their wisdom, lack a wise man. If there were such a person, he would bring into the Christian community the function sought in the civil courts.[22] Paul urges the Corinthian Christians to establish within the church not only the definition of justice (cf. Luke 12:57) but also the resolution of their contentions and difficulties.

Although Paul thinks it might be better if Christians would merely suffer wrong or be defrauded (6:7) he realizes that there are going to be contentions. Paul's solution: bring into the church the mechanisms that are operative in the world for adjudication of disputes.

Accordingly, in 2 Corinthians 13:1, where Paul projects another visit to Corinth, he lays down the well-established criterion by which his own disputes with them may be settled: "Any charge must be sustained by the evidence of two or three witnesses." But finally it must be stated that the Corinthians' judgments concerning Paul stand on a par with judgments rendered by civil courts: neither matters very much. "But with me it is a very small thing that I should be judged by you or by any human court. I do not even judge myself" (1 Cor. 4:3). God's judgment preempts human judgments and places them in proper perspective: "It is the Lord who judges me" (1 Cor. 4:4). Human institutions, even judgments made within the church by wise men on the basis of multiple witnesses, are all subsumed under the judgment of God. In the meantime, "before the Lord comes" (1 Cor.

4:5), human institutions and secular practices, subject to the judgment of God, may provide the models by which Christians can live together in Christ.[23]

Paul's eschatological view of the world and of God's judgment upon it was the ground on which he not only condemned the Corinthians' turning to the courts but also urged them to bring within the Christian community the world's means for adjudicating disputes. Accordingly, the Roman courts and their attendant legal system furnished patterns by which Paul could counsel his readers. The structures of the world, radically viewed in the light of God's judgment, provided some of the raw material out of which Paul fashioned his conceptualizations of Christian community and commitment.

Students of early Christianity have tended to overlook the plethora of organizations or associations present at the time of Christianity's beginning.[24] We could aptly call that the era of associations. To belong was a strong cultural drive and had been so since the disintegration of both the *polis* and the sense of identity it had offered. To counter insularity some people even resorted to memberships in several associations at the same time. Their choices were many: there were funeral associations, trade guilds, associations of farmers, herders, youths, or women, and other groups. This inclination to band together in associations and partnerships—an element in the "atmosphere of the age"— must be kept in view as we pursue our study.[25]

Paul employed a variety of metaphors and images to express the strong sense of community in Christ. Ernst Käsemann warns against a simplistic use of image or metaphor when applied to the church. He notes that too often scholars have conveyed the impression that the early Christians viewed "images of the church" as something akin to disembodied spirits isolated from "an actually existing reality."[26] We would extend Käsemann's point to include not only images and metaphors but also associations and transactions. When we see the early Christians conceptualizing

6

what it means to be brought into association with one another, we cannot lose sight of the social and historical matrix in which that community is established and understands itself. Everyday associations and transactions provided the means by which the early Christians could and did understand their new situation. Their shared life in Christ brought them into new relations with one another. Their relationships gained expression through recycled understandings of community taken from their social intercourse and dating from the time before they were Christians. To be sure, these understandings were more or less transformed under what the faithful experienced as the power of the good news in Christ, but the conceptualizations of community and commitment were never relegated to a vapid, extrahistorical level or stripped of their social and historical clothing.

In what follows we shall seek to identify the presence and assess the function of the Roman legal partnership, consensual *societas,* in portions of the Pauline letters.[27] Chapter 2 will profile consensual *societas.* In chapter 3 we will examine the connection of *societas* with the conference of Jerusalem (Gal. 2:1–10). The next chapter will disclose that Paul understood himself and the Philippian Christians to have *societas Christi,* partnership in Christ, together. Chapter 5 will ask whether there are signs of *societas* reflected elsewhere in the corpus of Pauline letters.[28] The final chapter will review the results and implications of this study.

NOTES

1. W. E. B. Ball, *St. Paul and the Roman Law* (Edinburgh: T. & T. Clark, 1901), pp. 36–37.
2. Cf. John C. Gager, *Kingdom and Community: The Social World of Early Christianity* (Englewood Cliffs, N.J.: Prentice Hall, 1975); Wayne A. Meeks, "The Social World of Early Christianity," *BullCSR* 6 (1975): 1; Jonathan Z. Smith, "The Social Description of Early Christianity," *RSR* 1 (1975): 19–21; and Abraham J. Malherbe, *Social*

Aspects of Early Christianity (Baton Rouge: Louisiana State University Press, 1977).

3. For a good summary of the range of evidence for Roman law from Cicero to the early third century c.e., see John Crook, *Law and Life of Rome* (Ithaca: Cornell University Press, 1967), esp. pp. 1–18 and footnotes. Cf. S. L. Sass, "Research in Roman Law: Guide to Sources," *LLJ* 56 (1963): 210–33. For an examination of some issues in Jewish and Roman law, cf. Boaz Cohen, *Jewish and Roman Law: A Comparative Study,* 2 vols. (New York: Jewish Theological Seminary of America, 1966).

4. Cf. Acts 16:37–39; 22:25–29; 23:27; 25:16; and 28:18.

5. See Gustave Bardy, "Saint Paul Juriste," *RechScRel* 31 (1943): 209–10, where he traces the tradition of calling Paul a jurisconsult all the way to one of Augustine's sermons and even sees a possible reflection of such a designation in the Muratorian Canon. I have not been able to gain access to an article that seems by title to promise more on this subject: Charles Boucaud, "Saint Paul Jurisconsulte," in the Catholic journal *La Question d'Israel* (Avril 1940): 83. That very year the journal apparently ceased publication.

6. For studies on slavery, see W. W. Buckland, *The Roman Law of Slavery* (Cambridge: Cambridge University Press, 1908); R. H. Barrow, *Slavery in the Roman Empire* (London: Methuen and Co., 1928); Crook, *Life of Rome,* pp. 179–92; A. H. M. Jones, "Slavery in the Ancient World," *EHR* 9 (1956): 185–99 (reprinted in M. I. Finley, ed., *Slavery in Classical Antiquity* [New York: Barnes & Noble, 1968]; Finley, *Slavery* (see the extensive bibliography, pp. 229–36); W. Brandt, *Dienst und Dienen im Neuen Testament* (Gütersloh: C. Bertelsmann, 1931); and *TDNT,* s.v. "*doulos.*"

7. See the considerable bibliography on this matter in F. Wilbur Gingrich and Frederick W. Danker, *A Greek-English Lexicon of the New Testament,* 2d ed. rev. (Grand Rapids: Zondervan Publishing House, 1979), p. 96.

8. See Stawros G. Huwardas, *Beiträge zum griechischen und gräko-ägyptischen Eherecht der Ptolemäer- und frühen Kaiserzeit* (Leipzig [Leipziger rechtswissenschaftliche Studien, 64]: T. Weicher, 1931); Gerhard Delling, "Ehescheidung," *RAC* 4:707–19.

9. Despite his rigorous demands for expertise in Roman law, Ball's chapter on adoption remains sweeping and generalizing: *St. Paul,* pp. 7–12.

10. Ibid., pp. 13–28; Otto Eger, "Rechtsworte und Rechtsbilder in

den paulischen Briefen," *ZNW* 18 (1917): 84–108; and Max Conrat, "Das Erbrecht im Galaterbrief (3,15–4,7)," *ZNW* 5 (1904): 204–27.

11. F. Lyall, "Roman Law in the Writings of Paul. Adoption," *JBL* 88 (1969): 458–66.

12. F. Lyall, "Roman Law in the Writings of Paul. The Slave and the Freedman," *NTS* 17 (1970): 73–79.

13. Greer M. Taylor, "The Function of *PISTIS CHRISTOU* in Galatians," *JBL* 85 (1966): 58–76. Taylor understands *fidei commissum* (a request by a testator that his heir use some inheritance in behalf of a third party) to explain how Abraham's inheritance is passed along to Jews and Greeks through Jesus Christ.) *14*

14. F. W. Danker, "Under Contract: A Form-Critical Study of Linguistic Adaptation in Romans," in *Festschrift to Honor F. Wilbur Gingrich*, ed. E. H. Barth and R. E. Cocroft (Leiden: E. J. Brill, 1972), pp. 91–114.

15. Peter Garnsey, *Social Status and Legal Privilege in the Roman Empire* (Oxford: Clarendon Press, 1970). Garnsey provides a good summary of his findings, beginning on p. 277.

16. Cf. James 2:6: "Is it not the rich who oppress you, is it not they who drag you into court?"

17. H. Strack and P. Billerbeck, *Kommentar zum Neuen Testament aus Talmud und Midrasch* (Munich: Beck, 1961), 3: 362–65; Jean Juster, *Les Juifs dans l'Empire romain* (Paris: P. Geuthner, 1914), 2: 110–11.

18. See Hans Conzelmann's accounting for Jewish avoidance of civil courts, *1 Corinthians*, trans. James W. Leitch (Philadelphia: Fortress Press, 1975), p. 104.

19. Contrast Mathias Delcor's reason for Paul's disappointment with the Corinthians on this matter. Delcor makes it seem more an exercise in public relations along the lines one reads in the pastoral epistles: "The Apostle wishes especially to prevent the private scandals of the *λε* community from being known by judges who did not share their faith." See "The Courts of the Church of Corinth and the Courts of Qumran," in *Paul and Qumran: Studies in New Testament Exegesis*, ed. J. Murphy-O'Connor (London: G. Chapman, 1968), p. 69.

20. Conzelmann, *1 Corinthians*, p. 104.

21. Erich Dinkler, "Zum Problem der Ethik bei Paulus: Rechtsnahme und Rechtsverzicht (1 Kor 6, 1–11)," *ZTK* 49 (1952): 167–200.

22. It could equally well be the case that Paul expected a group or

panel of wise men to be empowered to arbitrate. The way he puts the question concerning the *sophos* suggests: "Is there not even one?" (*outōs ouk eni en humin oudeis sophos*) (1 Cor. 6:5).

23. Cohen, *Jewish and Roman Law*, 1: 56: "Paul was eminently imbued with the culture of his day and was undoubtedly familiar with the current doctrines of Greek rhetoric and Roman law, which was natural for a man raised in Tarsus, the seat of a university where Stoic philosophy and Roman law were taught."

24. Classic treatments are J. -P. Waltzing, *Etude historique sur les corporations professionelles chez les Romains*, 4 vols. (Brussels: F. Hayez, 1895–96) and Franz Poland, *Geschichte des griechischen Vereinswesens* (Leipzig: B. G. Teubner, 1909). Cf. Wilhelm Liebenam, *Zur Geschichte und Organisation des römisches Vereinswesens* (Leipzig: B. G. Teubner, 1890). For a more modern treatment of associations in the Roman world see Ramsey MacMullen, *Roman Social Relations, 50* B.C. *to* A.D. *284* (New Haven: Yale University Press, 1974), pp. 57–87.

25. Cf. Robert L. Wilken, "Toward a Social Interpretation of Early Christian Apologetics," *CH* 39 (1970): 437–58 and MacMullen, *Roman Social Relations*, p. 77.

26. Ernst Käsemann, *Perspectives on Paul* (Philadelphia: Fortress Press, 1969), esp. pp. 101–5.

27. See my programmatic essay where I first set forward the findings that are the foundation for this monograph: "*Societas Christi:* Roman Law and Paul's Conception of the Christian Community," in *God's Christ and His People*, Festschrift in honor of Nils A. Dahl, ed. W. A. Meeks and J. Jervell (Oslo: Oslo University Press, 1977), pp. 158–74.

28. For our purposes, we will assume the authenticity of Romans, 1 and 2 Corinthians, Galatians, Philippians, 1 Thessalonians, and Philemon.

voluntary
binding - so long as agreed in good,
supported by social conscience
common goal
(matrimonium re: social states
each partner contributed something
a quasi-brotherhood

Very exciting

2

Consensual *Societas:*   I
Its Characteristic Features

Sometime in the opening decades of the first century B.C.E. a man
named Gaius Fannius Chaerea was sole owner of Panurgus, a
slave who early in his life showed great dramatic potential. Fannius contacted Quintus Roscius, a famous actor, and the two
agreed to enter a partnership along the following lines. Panurgus,
the slave, would become the slave of both Fannius and Roscius
if the latter would train him to become an actor. It was further
agreed that the two owners of the slave would split the profits
that Panurgus might earn. The legal apparatus by which this
agreement was realized was consensual *societas*, a prevalent
partnership contract of Roman law, where each of the partners
contributed something to the association with a view towards a
shared goal. The slave owner and the famous actor agreed to
attempt making a profit by contributing different things to the
partnership: the slave owner, half-interest in his slave; the pro-
fessional actor, his skills. To effect this agreement, the parties
needed no papers or public announcement. Simple agreement,
consent, was binding. We know about this *societas* because of
Cicero's involvement in litigation concerning it.

Fannius's perception of the slave's innate acting talent turned
out to be accurate because under Roscius's tutelage Panurgus became quite successful. Subsequently, however, the slave, Panurgus, was murdered by a Quintus Flavius. The actor sued Flavius
for the death of Panurgus; they settled out of court when Flavius

/u

X
general
partnership
to day the slave
would be the 3rd
party

11

gave Roscius, the actor, a farm as restitution for the death of Panurgus. Later the original slave owner, Fannius, sued Roscius for half the value of the farm since the settlement with the farm involved the partnership, the *societas*.[1] This complex incident reflects many of the characteristics of consensual *societas*.

The origins of *societas* are shrouded because of the relative lack of sources from ancient Greece Roman law around the time of Cicero and Paul knew of *societas* in several forms, whose roots may be traced back to a much older contract. The ancient partnership, *ercto non cito* (undivided inheritance), was a phenomenon of the family in which the father had died and the surviving sons inherited but did not divide the father's estate. Coming down through history to Roman times possibly from Babylonia, certainly from Greece, some form of partnership between heirs remained a possibility after the death of the head of the household. In Roman law this came to be called *societas omnium bonorum*, a partnership including the "whole property of all partners."[3]

In the partnerships *ercto non cito* and *societas omnium bonorum* only blood relatives could be involved.[4] If the primary heirs chose to include anyone outside the family a different arrangement had to be sought; *societas omnium bonorum* had to be terminated. Direct lineage, not any act of volition, is a basic feature of this ancient *societas* form.

Alongside *societas omnium bonorum*, and possibly patterned from it in some respects, there arose another *societas* whose membership depended not at all on common bloodline. Rather it called for consent between or among persons who had no necessary family relationship. It was an artificial consortium made up of persons who were drawn together by some mutually valued goal or purpose. It came to be known as consensual *societas* and is the form that will concern us in this study.[5]

Already in the second century B.C.E. consensual *societas* was well known. It was termed *koinōnia* in the Greek.[7] Closer to the time of the Apostle Paul, Cicero knew consensual *societas* and

12

clearly distinguished it from the older, hereditary form: "Did
you form a voluntary partnership [*voluntariam societatem*] with
the man who had cheated you in an hereditary partnership
[*hereditaria societate*]?" (*Pro Quinctio* 76).

At the turn of the eras consensual *societas* was prevalent as a
legally binding, reciprocal partnership or association, freely
entered upon between one person and one or more other persons
regarding a particular goal or shared concern. The shared goal—
for example, making a profit via Panurgus as in our opening story
—was the focal point. People of diverse economic and social
backgrounds might be drawn together into *societas* by the mutual
valuation of a particular aim.[9] Their common focus on the shared
goal—not similar backgrounds or social standing—provided the
basis for their unity. Though the aim of most *societates* was
clearly financial, such need not be the case.[10]

Voluntary *societas* was one of four contracts in Roman law that
were termed consensual. The other three were sale (*venditio*),
hire (*locatio conductio*), and mandate (*mandatum*). All four
were "uniquely Roman" in that nothing more than agreement of
the parties—no matter how it is expressed—was required to
initiate the contract.[11] No property need change hands. Likewise
no money had to be exchanged.[12]

Consensual *societas* required neither witnesses nor written documents nor notification of authorities.[13] Simple agreement was all
that was required.[14] The *societas* was in effect from the moment
of that accord. Consensual *societas* ought not to be viewed as a
casual undertaking, however. The *societas* partners entered into
a legally binding contract whose terms could be subject to court
tests and public sanction. Merely owning property together did
not constitute consensual *societas*. A consensual *societas* oper-
ated when partners agreed to use property or labor in common
towards a particular goal that was beyond the property or labor
itself.

Each of the parties to consensual *societas* contributed to the
partnership one or more of the following: property, labor, skill,

or status. In the earlier Ciceronian example Fannius, the slave owner, contributed half-ownership of the slave, Panurgus; Roscius gave instruction in acting. The terms of the partnership could be adjusted in any way agreeable to the partners, with one exception: it was not permitted to say that one partner was liable for losses alone but ineligible for profits.[15] No matter what one contributed to the partnership, one was to share whatever profits or losses came to the *societas*. Even in cases where profit was not the object of consensual *societas* there was still a "common exploitation of capital or labour for a common purpose."[16]

Once the partners reached agreement, they were bound to act according to the terms of the agreement. They were to contribute what they had promised. There were no hard and fast rules determining how the partners were to comport themselves toward each other. A clue concerning the general guidelines of the care one ought to show in *societas* may be recovered by the knowledge that court suits brought concerning *societas* were considered *bona fide* not *stricti iuris* (governed by strict rules).[17] In the latter no allowance was made for mitigating circumstances. In *stricti iuris* cases the judicial formula went: "If it appears that X owes . . . [and has not paid] then condemn."[18] With *societas*, however, the lawsuit was *bona fide*. There the judge "must decide 'what in all fairness the defendant ought to pay or do.'"[19]

No partner was free to turn the *societas* to his own ends or to use the *societas* to advance himself at the expense of the other partners. Rather the foundation of *societas* was mutual trust and reciprocity. The good of all the partners must be served by the actions of the individual partner (*socius*). "The reciprocal confidence, honesty, good faith of the parties" was fundamental "at both the conclusion of the accord and the execution of the assumed duties."[20] The emphasis on consent was a hallmark of *societas* from start to finish. "Apparently any *socius* might veto an administrative proposal of any or all the others so as to make persistence in it a wrong."[21] Once more the partners are equals. No one coerces the others. The others do not compel the individual.

14

Consensual *Societas:* Its Characteristic Features

When under way, the *societas* endured as long as the mutual trust continued and as long as the partners remained committed to the common purpose that brought them together in the first place. Gaius, though a man of the second century C.E., codified the legal traditions inherited from prior times and wrote: "A partnership [*societas*] lasts as long as the parties remain of the same mind [*in eodem sensu*]."[22] To be "of the same mind" is a shorthand way of saying that the aim of the *societas* remains central and functional for the partners.

One or more of the partners might undertake special roles in service of the *societas'* interests. The undertakings of such a representative were clearly circumscribed. His actions were governed by and should conform to the goal that occasioned the *societas*. He could do business for the *societas*, under its direction and in keeping with its goal, but he was not, strictly and legally speaking, an agent of the *societas* to acquire something or to enter into further partnerships. If he did make some purchase or enter into another contemporaneous partnership—which he could do on his own initiative—then he had no power to bind his original partners. In that sense he was not their agent. He could function as a representative of the *societas*, however, if he did what the *societas* had agreed he should do. Any *socius,* partner, who undertook to represent the *societas* was entitled to remuneration "for expenses properly incurred."[23] Accounting for expenses and disbursements could be required of the *socius*.

Provided reciprocity and mutual trust were maintained, the duration of a particular *societas* was determined in large measure by the scope of the goal that brought the partnership into being. The *societas* could be undertaken for a very specific task of either short or long range, or it could be entered into for a more general goal that could take either a short or long time to accomplish. Again the goal determined the duration of the contract; when it was accomplished the *societas* was naturally terminated.

Premature termination of *societas* was quite possible, however. The death of one of the partners dissolved the partnership unless some provision in that regard had been made in advance. How-

15

ever, the surviving partners (*socii*) could constitute another *societas* around the same goal. *Societas* also ended prematurely when any partner lost commitment to the original goal or aim. When that person was no longer "of the same mind" then the *societas* dissolved. Likewise "renunciation by a partner always ended the partnership."[24] Just as surely as the contract originated consensually, one could withdraw from it at will, the exception being when one could see the *societas* about to suffer great loss. Because *societas* was so dependent on mutual trust of the partners, fraud or deceit would also prematurely end *societas*. The term most often used to describe such a violation of *societas* was *dolus*, "any cunning, deceit, or contrivance used to defraud, deceive or cheat another."[25]

Societas was subject to enforcement in the courts (*actio pro socio*). When matters became so bad that *societas* reached the courtroom, it had effectively terminated, but satisfaction could be sought. Settlement of disputes over *societas* were sometimes pursued in the civil courts—as in our opening example—but the *societas* must be understood as no longer vital at that stage. By the very nature of *societas*, when partners take one another to court they can no longer be characterized as being "of the same mind."

One could not take the ultimate sanction of the courts lightly, however, because conviction in an *actio pro socio* brought the verdict of *infamia*. This punishment was severe in two major ways: First, it branded one in the eyes of the community as unworthy of the "overt esteem" (*existimatio, dignitas*) sought so dearly.[26] Second, this peer rejection spilled over into the limitations of one's rights in the closely knit society. The person guilty of *infamia* lost certain rights in the courts.[27]

It should be readily apparent that partnerships (*societates*) at the turn of the eras are quite distinct from modern corporations. *Societates* have no legal personality, no corporate identity. They are considerably less complex but incredibly more fragile. Their frailty is derived from at least two features: the paucity of regulations and guidelines concerning appropriate action and the

16

occasional human desire to make personal gain at the expense of others. Counterbalancing that fragile character of *societas*, however, is a strong sense of obligation to keep one's word. Also there is the concern for one's personal standing in the community. "The special characteristic of Roman as compared with modern society in this regard is usually said to have been that the security they gave and took was comparatively rarely 'real' security (money or land or other objects of value) and comparatively frequently 'personal' security, that is, the personal standing and credit of their friends and patrons brought in as a guarantee of their own transactions."[28] The social fabric of these times was closely woven; the pattern of personal obligation must be seen in that context.

From a sociological standpoint, *societas* is unique in Roman law. As severely stratified as Roman society was, *societas* allowed persons of different social strata to become equal partners with one another. In fact, most strikingly, even slaves, who according to Roman law are generally recognized to have no legal standing in other regards, could become full partners (*socii*) in a *societas* with persons of any rank.[29] Consider the *Digest* 17.2.58.3:

> If a slave of mine enters into partnership with Titius, and is then disposed of to some one else, but continues in the same partnership, it is a fair construction that by the transfer of the slave the old partnership is terminated and another one started afresh, so that there is a good right of action *pro socio* both for me and the purchaser, and that an action will also be allowed against me and the purchaser equally in respect of such grounds of action as occurred before the transfer was made, but in respect of all other grounds against the purchaser only.[30]

Furthermore, the ancient roots of *societas* in the family unit, in which those who were literally brothers inherited the goods of the deceased father, continue to mark even consensual *societas*: a quasi-brotherly relationship was understood to exist among partners no matter what their social standing might be.[31]

In what follows we shall see a range of ways in which the very popular and adaptable Roman contract, consensual *societas*, was used by Paul in his letters.

NOTES

1. The details of this particular contract are found in Cicero *Pro Roscio Comoedo*.

2. Emile Szlechter, *Le Contrat de Société en Babylonie, en Grèce, et à Rome* (Paris: Recueil Sirey, 1947), traces the roots of this ancient partnership back into Babylonian times.

3. Adolf Berger, *Encyclopedic Dictionary of Roman Law*, Transactions of the American Philosophical Society, N. S. 43, 2 (Philadelphia: American Philosophical Society, 1953), p. 709.

4. Ibid., p. 455.

5. Alan Watson, *The Law of Obligations in the Later Roman Republic* (Oxford: Clarendon Press, 1965), p. 41. So also David Daube, "Societas as a Consensual Contract," *CLJ* 6 (1938): 381–403.

6. "Such a consensual partnership must have been recognized in Rome long before the passing of the *lex Aebutia* [ca. 2d century B. C. E.] and before the time when the formulary system was thought to have been introduced." Alan Watson, "Consensual *Societas* Between Romans and the Introduction of Formulae," *RIDA* 9 (1962): 434. Cf. Szlechter, *Le Contrat de Société.*

7. J. W. Jones, *The Law and Legal Theory of the Greeks* (Oxford: Clarendon Press, 1956), p. 163. *Koinōnia* is "ambiguous" when referred to Greek associations. For more extensive evidence on *koinōnia* as the analog for *societas* see below, chap. 3, n. 26.

8. Cf. Michael Wegner, *Untersuchungen zu der lateinischen Begriffen socius und societas* (Göttingen: Vandenhoeck & Ruprecht, 1969), p. 27: "Die durch *socius* ausgedrückte Beziehung zwischen Personen wird also en einer gemeinsamen Aktion oder Reaktion gegenüber aussenstehenden Personen oder Dingen festgestellt, nicht— wie e.g. bei *comes, amicus, minister*—an dem Verhalten der einen Person, des *socius*, gegenüber der anderen."

9. Francis de Zulueta, *The Institutes of Gaius*, pt. 2 (Oxford: Clarendon Press, 1953), p. 179, n. 3.

10. *Societas* "includes any agreement for the common exploitation of capital or labour for a common purpose, whether that purpose be profit or not." H. F. Jolowicz, *Historical Introduction to the Study of Roman Law* (Cambridge: Cambridge University Press, 1965), p. 309.

11. Alan Watson, *The Law of the Ancient Romans* (Dallas: Southern Methodist University Press, 1970), p. 66.

12. As compared with Jewish law, a distinctive feature of Roman law emerges here. Cf. George Horowitz, *The Spirit of Jewish Law*

Consensual *Societas:* Its Characteristic Features

(New York: Central Book Co., 1953), p. 447 (italics his): "But the other two [contracts]: the *verbal* . . . and the *consensual* based upon *consensus,* agreement only, were hardly known in Jewish law." Unlike the consensual *societas* of Roman law, the following prevails in Jewish law: "According to an early and basic principle, a partnership cannot be formed by words alone whether spoken or written. There must be a transfer of property or at least *kinyan* (i.e., a simulated transfer) in order to establish a partnership" (p. 557).

13. Watson, *Law of Obligations,* p. 128.

14. Szlechter, *Le Contrat de Société,* p. 129.

15. "Indeed the whole risk of loss might be put on one *socius* in the sense that he was to provide all the capital and the other only work; but obviously the latter risked throwing away his contribution of valuable work." Zulueta, *Institutes of Gaius,* pt. 2, p. 179.

16. Jolowicz, *Historical Introduction,* p. 309.

17. "The concept of *bona fides* and all its associated ideas were all Roman in origin and represent a considerable original creation of Roman juristic thought. Still there is no doubt that the Aristotelian ideas, and their Stoic counterparts, had their own impact." Moshe Shagli, "Aristotle's Concept of Responsibility and its Reflection in Roman Jurisprudence," *ILR* 6 (1971): 64.

18. John Crook, *Law and Life of Rome* (Ithaca: Cornell University Press, 1967), p. 208.

19. Ibid., p. 82.

20. Berger, *Roman Law,* p. 374.

21. W. W. Buckland, *A Text-book of Roman Law from Augustus to Justinian* (Cambridge: Cambridge University Press, 1921), p. 506.

22. Gaius 3. 151; Zulueta, *Institutes of Gaius,* pt. 1, p. 201.

23. Buckland, *Text-book of Roman Law,* p. 506.

24. Watson, *Law of Obligations,* p. 133.

25. Berger, *Roman Law,* p. 440. Cf. *Digest* 4.3.1.2.

26. Crook, *Life of Rome,* p. 83.

27. Ibid., p. 84. Cf. Gaius 4. 182; Zulueta, *Institutes of Gaius,* pt. 2, p. 300, where the latter acknowledges: "*Infamia* was not a sharply defined legal concept, but covered a variety of cases, statutory as well as edictal." See A. H. J. Greenidge, *Infamia: Its Place in Roman Public and Private Law* (Oxford: Clarendon Press, 1894).

28. Crook, *Life of Rome,* p. 243.

29. Alan Watson, "Illogicality and Roman Law," *ILR* 7 (1972): 19.

30. Translation and text from C. H. Monro, ed. and trans., *Digest* 17.2 *Pro Socio* (Cambridge: Cambridge University Press, 1902), pp.

44–45. Si servus meus societatem cum Titio coierit et alienatus in eadem permanserit, potest dici alienatione servi et priorem societatem finitam et ex integro alteram inchoatam, atque ideo et mihi et emptori actionem pro socio competere, item tam adversus me quam adversus emptorem ex his causis quae ante alienationem inciderunt dandam actionem, ex reliquis adversus emptorem solum.

31. Barry Nicholas, *An Introduction to Roman Law* (Oxford: Clarendon Press, 1962), p. 186, and Zulueta, *Institutes of Gaius,* pt. 2, p. 179, n. 3, speak respectively of the " 'brotherly' character of the contract" and that the partners become "quasi-brothers."

3

Paul's View of the Jerusalem Conference

If Paul had not been in a dispute with some people in Galatia concerning the importance and purpose of his visits to Jerusalem, we would not have his accounting of what went on at the conference in Jerusalem. To be sure, we would have Luke's version in Acts 15, but that provides no real access to Paul's own perception of the meeting. We would in fact be left to discern from Paul's other letters his understanding of how Gentiles could become Christians without becoming Jews, without being circumcised. We would also have a considerable puzzle concerning the appearance in Romans, in 1 Corinthians, and again, even massively, in 2 Corinthians of discussions and appeals concerning "remembering the poor" or "the offering for the saints" in Jerusalem. And, perhaps most puzzling of all, we would read Romans on this matter and see that Paul was going to deliver that offering or collection to Jerusalem in spite of known personal peril (Rom. 15:25–33). After the collection is delivered Paul's own accounts become silent; his letters stop. Acts picks up the story and gives us reason to believe Paul's fears were well grounded. He was arrested in Jerusalem. Acts carries the case forward as Paul appeals to ever higher tribunals.

In these matters of the collection, its delivery, and Paul's subsequent arrest, Acts again could be of no aid in disclosing Paul's motivation. In fact, Acts would not help us understand the collection at all unless we mistakenly identified the type of offering noted in Acts 11:30 with the Pauline collection.[1] There is, however, sufficient evidence to cause all these matters to fall into place. It is found in Paul's defense of himself against the Galatian rumors and claims. His account to the Galatians of the conference in Jerusalem lets us know how he viewed that meeting, its significance and its outcome.

In the fire of controversy with the Galatians, Paul recounts the extent of his contact with the leaders of the church in Jerusalem, the pillars from among the original disciples.[2] Before the conference at Jerusalem, Paul contends that he had been to Jerusalem only once—and that for only a fortnight. He had visited with Peter and seen James—but none of the other apostles. Thus there could be no assertion that he received authorization from the original disciples.[3] That claim is punctuated by an oath (Gal. 1:20).

Paul tells the Galatians that the only other visit he ever made to Jerusalem was for the conference. He tells them about the conference not because he assumes they have a burning interest in it but because he is in part saying what he did *not* do there. He is clearing himself from the charge that his gospel was derivative, secondhand, learned at the feet of or authenticated by the original apostles. So Paul is saying his second visit could not possibly be construed as the source of instruction or apostolic authorization. Rather at the Jerusalem conference Paul laid out the evidence of God's grace already at work in his ministry over the past several years. And he is quick to point out that the Jerusalem apostles recognized God's grace at work (2:9).[5]

There are several noteworthy features of Paul's version of the conference (Gal. 2:1–10) that bear on our study.[6] But first some general observations must be made as necessary background. According to Paul, his presence at the conference was not dictated by the order of some Christian community; neither was he there in response to a summons from the Jerusalem apostles. Indeed,

22

he attended the conference not even by his own will. He went up
to Jerusalem "by revelation" (2:2). The meeting was generated
not by human willing; it was brought about by God instructing
him through a revelation. Thus Paul transfers it from the arena
of contending forces or ideas to a working out of God's will. Interpreters who would see the conference as a showdown have not
sufficiently weighed this opening feature of Paul's account.

Paul goes to the conference not as a novice in the preaching of
the gospel. He has preached it for several years (perhaps as
many as fourteen or seventeen) and has established Christian
congregations across a considerable geographic area.[8] As Paul describes the conference, it reaches its turning point when James,
Cephas, and John "perceived the grace that was given to me"
(2:9)[9] When that grace is known (gnontes) they give Paul and
Barnabas the "right hand of fellowship." Though it is not said in
so many words, it is clearly God's grace that the "pillars" come to
perceive as at work in Paul, just as it has been God's revelation
that caused Paul to go to Jerusalem. The "grace at work in Paul"
may have become apparent by some manifestation performed at
the conference itself, but more likely it was the witness to God's
grace provided by a report of the faith of the Pauline Christian
communities across the northeastern quarter of the Mediterranean world.

Throughout his correspondence, Paul uses the term grace or
grace of God as the mark of his work in Christ.[10] For example, he
tells the Romans that he has written to them "very boldly . . .
because of the grace given me by God to be a minister of Christ
Jesus to the Gentiles in the priestly service of the gospel of God"
(Rom. 15:15–16). It is God's grace that has empowered him to be
a minister among the Gentiles so that they might be an acceptable offering, sanctified by the Holy Spirit (15:16). As Paul indicates in several of his other letters, the Gentiles' faith, elicited in
response to his preaching, has been infectious among other Gentiles (1 Thess. 1:8; Philem. 5). Their faith has gone out beyond

23

their communities and has encouraged others. Now Paul tells the Galatians that the faith of the Gentile Christians had reached even the Jerusalem pillars, and the latter saw it as God's grace at work in Paul's preaching among the Gentiles.

In Paul's recollection, the Jerusalem conference climaxed in a very specific action, initiated by James, Cephas, and John: they gave Paul and Barnabas "the right hand of fellowship" (2:9).

It is probably safe to aver that no other single event in the first century of Christianity is more important for the survival and shaping of the Christian tradition and practice than this conference at Jerusalem in the mid-first century. We are fortunate enough to have Paul's own understanding of its inception and the manner in which it came to a conclusion. It is precisely in its conclusion that interpreters have encountered some uncertainty concerning Paul's meaning. The pillars of the Jerusalem church, seeing God's grace in Paul's preaching, gave the right hand to Paul and Barnabas. Obviously some form of unity is symbolized by that action. Some agreement is signaled. What has been a matter of scholarly dispute and confusion has been the precise relationship symbolized by the ones giving the right hand to the others. It is a symbolic action, but what are the relationships among those five people and the groups they represent?[11] Are the three Jerusalem pillars welcoming Paul and Barnabas as equals? As subordinates? Are Paul and Barnabas, in the receiving of the right hand, acknowledging the superiority of the pillars? Or are Barnabas and Paul receiving them as equals? Further, are Paul and Barnabas simply the recipients of the given right hand? Or do they in some sense also give their own right hands in the matter? What were the actual terms and nature of the agreement symbolized in the giving of the right hand? The text itself aids us in answering what some of the terms of the agreement were (2:10), but that still leaves unanswered the question of their force. Who pledged what to whom? An accurate assessment of the significance of that conference for early Christianity rests in part

24

on our capacity to answer some or all of these questions with precision.

PREVIOUS EFFORTS TO UNDERSTAND "GIVING OF THE RIGHT HAND"

Interpreters have for some time recognized that *dexias edōkan*,[12] "gave the right hand," was formulaic and technical, but there has been no certainty or agreement concerning what it signified.[13] Lightfoot, in his 1896 commentary, noted the formulaic phrase and suggested the rather neutral "gave pledges."[14] Lightfoot and many after him noted the nearest parallels in Israel's traditions were passages such as Lamentations 5:6 and 2 Chronicles 30:8, where *ntn yd* signified "to surrender." Lightfoot observed that "the giving of the right hand . . . was a recognized pledge of fidelity with other Eastern nations, with the Persians especially."[15] There is nothing in Galatians 2:1–10 to suggest that "surrender" is involved on either side, so Lightfoot settles for "gave pledges." What was pledged? What were the terms on which the pledges were made? What was the force of them? As right as Lightfoot is that *dexias edōkan* is a technical phrase, we are still no closer to answers for these questions.[16]

Burton widens the evidence from Israel's traditions as he tries to understand the giving of the right hand at the Jerusalem conference. On the basis of his examination of the evidence, he rules out surrender or submission and opts for "a pledge of friendship": "In none of these cases [1 Macc. 6:58, 11:50, 62, 66, 13:50, 2 Macc. 11:26, 12:11, 13:22; Josephus, *Ant.* 18.328 (9:3); 20.62 (3:2)] does the giving of the hand indicate submission, but a pledge of friendship."[17] Though the "pledge of friendship" attempts to specify the content of the pledges, and therefore moves beyond Lightfoot, the phrase does not communicate a great deal. Burton goes ahead to develop the relationship symbolized by the giving of the right hand. In his examples from Israel's traditions, Burton notices a pattern: the pledge of friendship is "in most cases from the superior power to the inferior."[18] If Burton is right and the proffering of right hand is made by the superior to the inferior, then we have come a distance in answering some of our questions about the precise relationship with the Jerusalem pillars that Paul understands to have eventuated from the conference at Jerusalem. According to this interpretation, the pillars, by their giving of the right hand to Barnabas and Paul, exercised their authority over the latter. Can one suppose that the latter, by receiving the right hand, affirmed the superiority of the pillars? The entire thrust of the material in Galatians prior to the Jerusalem conference account argues against such a superior-inferior interpretation. From the salutation, where Paul declares his apostleship is not through human authority but from Jesus Christ and God (1:1), to the account of the conference itself Paul shows himself answerable only to God and Christ. Paul declares that the pillars "added nothing to me" (2:6). He point-blank denies that he has yielded in submission to any outsiders (2:5). In fact, the *opponents* of Paul in Galatia seem to be arguing along the lines of Burton's interpretation of "giving of the right hand." But Paul insists there was no dependence on the Jerusalem church leaders. Therefore the interpretation of superior-inferior for the giving and receiving of right hands seems patently out of joint with the context. Of course, Paul is capable of the fool's modesty, such as he shows in 2 Corinthians where he can talk about those "superlative apostles" (11:5 and 12:11). But Paul shows no signs of that ironic rhetoric in his account of the Jerusalem conference. He simply reports that the Jerusalem leaders, when they saw God's grace at work in Paul and Barnabas, gave them the right hand.

A NEW LOOK AT GALATIANS 2:9

Despite the past interpretive efforts, Galatians 2:9 does provide the necessary clues for unraveling its meaning. When we look back upon such a watershed event and try to assess every detail for its significance, we sometimes lose sight of the everyday forms in which human transactions—no matter how important or lofty—are realized. Later we may come to see the fuller significance and even load those everyday transactions with symbolism appropriate to the significance we have subsequently come to see them have. The Jerusalem conference brought together the main leaders of the young, pluralistic church. As Paul saw it a consensus developed there. The parties exchanged right hands and emerged with a single mission, one group headed toward the Jews, the other toward the Gentiles. In that moment where consensus was realized, what transpired with the giving of the right hand?

Past scholarly efforts at understanding "giving of the right hand" have failed because they have looked simply to Israel's traditions. That has been the weakness of Burton. The Jerusalem conference occurs because Israel—and the sectarian messianic movement that began within it—is not hermetically sealed off from the Greco-Roman world around it. Do Greeks have to become Jews to become Christians? That is the focal issue of the conference. In an analogous fashion, when the consensus develops among the early Christian leaders, one need not expect the newfound unity to be symbolized purely and simply in ritual actions specific to Israel. The giving of the right hand may simply be a symbolic action common to people across the Greco-Roman world —whether those people be Jews or Gentiles. And so it is in fact.

Dexias didonai, the giving of the right hand, is attested in the papyri for three centuries before and two centuries after the Jerusalem conference as a solemn sealing of a contract with the person or persons involved.[19] To "give the right hand" is to enter into a contract with someone. Likewise, in the literature of the time, to "keep the right hand" or "guard the right hand" is the rhetoric of contract performance.[20] When a question of faithfulness to a contract arises one may be asked whether he is keeping or guarding his right hand.

There is an understandable reticence to view such lofty and historic events in the early life of the church in terms of the mundane. But the Jerusalem conference is after all a transaction among men who can ritualize those transactions in the ways the culture has provided them. Lightfoot in 1896 already saw the limitations of his search for illuminating background materials to help him understand the giving of the right hand at the Jerusalem conference. The giving of the right hand, Lightfoot acknowledged, as a "symbol of contract or friendship . . . does not appear prominently in the Old Testament . . . nor is it especially Jewish."[21] No, but the *hellenistic* literature shows that giving the right hand is the making of a contract or agreement. In fact, it can even be the making of a contract that is enforceable by legal constraints. Consider one example that illustrates many of the points at issue here. A second century C.E. man named Theogiton writes a certain Apollonius. In part the papyrus letter says: "Indeed you appear to me to be quite mad this month in not keeping your pledge [*mē phylass*]*i*[*n sou tēn dexian*, literally, not keeping your right hand], since even if there were no documents, still, thank heaven, there is no preconceived principle on our part that should make you suppose that we will be illegally ousted" (*P. Fay.* 124.11–24). At issue is Apollonius's monthly support of his mother. From this document it is possible to reconstruct that Apollonius has given his right hand to his mother concerning that support. Theogiton writes Apollonius and threatens legal action to enforce performance of the contract. The absence of documents is no hindrance. Apollonius's giving of his right hand binds him to the agreement; he must keep the right hand. Other papyri confirm that the giving of the right hand commences contracts, enacts formal agreements.[22]

The papyri enable us to advance our understanding of the conclusion of the Jerusalem conference—as Paul viewed it. Fully in line with the force of the material in chapter 1 of Galatians, Paul and Barnabas do not surrender or submit themselves to the Jerusalem pillars. Neither does Paul report that the conference ended with some vague pledges of friendship.[23] Rather he reports to his Galatian readers that the meeting ended in a formal agreement, a solemn contract with the Jerusalem pillars.[24] This contract binds him and Barnabas on the one side with Peter, James, and John on the other. Whatever the precise nature of the agreement or contract, it called for a division of labor: the pillars devoting their attention to the circumcised, Paul and Barnabas going to the Gentiles.

Though the papyri enable us to see that the meeting ended in a formal agreement or contract, we know that agreements and contracts came in many forms, with widely varied terms. Different contracts entailed different responsibilities and brought the contracting parties together on different terms. Without knowing what particular type of agreement was involved one would neither know the structure of the contract nor its parameters.

But Paul tells the reader directly what type of agreement is involved. He reports that the Jerusalem pillars gave him and Barnabas the right hand "of fellowship [koinōnia]" (2:9).[25] Not every appearance of the term koinōnia is equivalent to the Latin societas. In the papyri, as in Paul's letters, the term has a range of uses, one of which is to specify the particular agreement known in Roman law as societas.[26] In the Galatian account of the conference, "giving of the right hand" is the decisive clue that we are confronted with a binding agreement; the appearance of koinōnia in association with it may be understood as a genitive of description or specification, clarifying what particular contract or agreement was involved among the five leaders of the early church gathered in Jerusalem.[27] It was societas as Paul understood it, an actual—not simply metaphorical—commitment, a formal obligation.

Whatever may have been Luke's view of the consummation of the Jerusalem conference, Paul understands that the meeting eventuated in a consensual societas, a partnership among the major leaders of the church. What was the goal around which the partnership coalesced? It was the joint preaching of the one gospel: "that we should go to the Gentiles and they to the circumcised" (2:9).[28] As Paul viewed it the Jerusalem pillars acknowledged God's grace at work in Paul's preaching. By the means of a consensual partnership contract, they all recognized their brotherhood in Christ and joined together in the common task of preaching the gospel.

The point is not that the five leaders set up business together in some commercial sense. Rather as they shared the results of Paul's years of preaching, they came to realize their true brotherhood in Christ. There were not two gospels; only one. And they were all already preaching it. The brotherhood they discovered in the Jerusalem conference gained expression and was symbolized by the giving and receiving of the right hand of *societas*. From that conference they could each go out as representatives of the same gospel with a division of labor, not a parting of the ways.

The *societas* they formalized with the giving of the right hand did not eliminate all distinctive features or differences among the newfound partners. Unity, not uniformity, resulted. The brotherhood of the new partners does not exist because of some precontract disposition or affection towards each other; nor does it eliminate future struggles. Their newfound unity comes about because each party recognizes a common purpose at work among them. Therefore these diverse people join together in Jerusalem for the shared goal of preaching the gospel and, in the process, affirm the unity of God's work among both Jews and Gentiles.

Paul insists to the Galatians that his partnership came about without his yielding to the pillars and without their adding anything to him (2:6). In 2:10, however, we see that one condition was laid upon him and Barnabas as part of the *societas*: "Only they would have us remember the poor." Verse 10 is introduced with *monon*, "only," in a position of emphasis, indicating that no other requirements or specifications were laid down by the pillars.

Syntactically 2:10 hangs on the previous verse. It is the second of two clauses that specify the details of the contract.[29] The first clause expresses the division of labor in preaching the gospel: we to the Gentiles, they to the circumcised (2:9).[30] The second clause (2:10) discloses a condition that the pillars laid on Paul and Barnabas from the very start, as part of the terms of the original pact. They are to remember the poor. So Paul and Barnabas come away from the Jerusalem conference with two tasks: they are to preach the gospel to the Gentiles—something they were already doing but now can continue to do with the conviction that they are not at odds with their Jerusalem-based brothers in Christ —and they are to take up a collection for the poor in Jerusalem.[31]

The laconic statement "remember the poor" is one of the many points where the modern reader is at a distinct disadvantage when compared with the original readers for whom the document was intended.[32] One can in fact surmise that Paul had trouble with the Galatian churches not only over circumcision and its relation to the gospel but also concerning their participation in the stipulated collection. One can deduce that because, in Romans, where Paul declares himself ready to depart for Rome with a projected stopover in Jerusalem to deliver the collection, Paul notes several areas from which the collection has been gathered, and Galatia is conspicuous in its absence (Rom. 15:26). The Galatians know what remembering the poor is. Paul (Gal. 2:10) reminds them that it was part of the Jerusalem partnership from the very start.

There is no clue—in Galatians or elsewhere in the corpus— whether Paul and Barnabas put any special requirements on the Jerusalem pillars. In and of itself *societas* did not entail counter-requirements. Different partners could be expected to contribute differently to the partnership. That remembering the poor was required does not alter the equality of the *societas* partners. Perhaps he and Barnabas laid counter-requirements on the pillars; there is simply no way for us to know. It should be borne in mind, however, that Paul relates this information about the Jerusalem conference not in the interests of complete historical record but in order to counter specific Galatian charges that have been brought against him.

Paul concludes his account of the Jerusalem conference by asserting that remembering the poor was an undertaking for which Paul had a great zeal anyway. Is this empty rhetoric, designed to minimize the requirement that was imposed by others? If so a rationalizing paraphrase might read: "It is not so bad to have to do this since I was already somewhat interested in it." However, the treatment of the collection in the Letter to the Romans makes clear that Paul saw a theological appropriateness to it; in fact, he viewed it as an obligation that the Gentiles owed. It was a debt.[33] And it should be paid off with cheerfulness. The Corinthians were right to undertake it with enthusiasm (2 Cor. 8:10). The Macedonians had joined in as well (Rom. 15:26).[34] As Paul prepares to deliver it to Jerusalem and thereby fulfill his obligation undertaken a couple of years earlier at the conference, he tells the Romans of its preparation and significance: "They [Macedonia and Achaia] were pleased to do it [take part in the collection], and indeed they are in debt to them, for if the Gentiles have come to share in their spiritual blessings, they ought also to be of service to them in material blessings" (Rom. 15:27). Paul affirms the dependent status of the Gentiles in God's plan. The Jews have always been God's people first. Paul knows that and refines the idea into what amounts to a refrain in Romans: "the Jew first; also the Greek" (Rom. 1:16; 2:9, 10). When it comes to matters of the church, Paul recognizes a priority of the Jewish Christians and that Gentile Christians are becoming recipients of the blessings that belonged first to the Jews. The Gentile Christians are therefore placed in the debt of the Jewish Christians. Paul sees that this has taken place in Christ without the Gentile Christians becoming second-class citizens. Nevertheless the Gentile Christians must recognize that God's grace has come to them, allowing them to share what was initially promised only to Israel. Gentile Christians are therefore at one and the same time debtors to their Jewish Christian brothers and sisters as well as equal sharers with them of God's grace.

It is not unreasonable to suppose that there was a pressing need for relief in Jerusalem.[35] But it is a striking confirmation of our claim here that Paul's appeal concerning the collection is never once predicated on the dire straits of the Jerusalem Christians or on any suffering there. The appeal is not based on pity for others but on grateful response for what has been received without merit.

Quite appropriately, in this Galatian letter known for its great emphasis on freedom, Paul's eagerness to do what is at the same time required of him offers an insight into Paul's understanding of Christian freedom.[36] Does the necessity of the collection rob Paul of his freedom in Christ? Not at all. His freedom can be exercised in doing the very thing required of him. Further, the fact that it is a requirement does not dull his eagerness about it. No empty rhetoric here. No modern notion that freedom must be the absence of restraints. On the contrary, Paul knows his freedom in Christ enables him to undertake joyously even some things that are required of him. In his freedom, he fully wants to do the very thing that the Jerusalem pillars require. As matters turned out, Paul appears to have been clearer on this interplay of freedom and obligation than some of his congregations were.

Our discovery that Paul views the Jerusalem conference as climaxing with the formation of a consensual *societas*, a partnership for preaching the gospel, enables us to answer more carefully some of the questions raised earlier. By his own declaration Paul makes clear that the agreement reached in Jerusalem was a *koinōnia*, a *societas*. We know from the extant literature and records that *societas* was a consensual contract. By definition no one could compel another into consensual *societas*. Paul's account of the Jerusalem conference is fully in line with that: the Jerusalem pillars are not forced into partnership with Paul and Barnabas; neither is the opposite the case. Paul is careful to say that the Jerusalem pillars freely made the first move towards partnership when they came to realize that God's grace was truly at work in Paul and Barnabas.

No *societas* is formed until there is a goal or purpose around which the interested parties focus. There must be a common goal to which all the people commit themselves. Paul's account of the Jerusalem conference, though quite cryptically stated, makes it clear that the shared goal about which the Jerusalem *societas* coalesced was the preaching of the gospel: "We should go to the Gentiles and they to the circumcised" (2:9).

The Jerusalem *societas* confirms what we must suppose to have been the preconference practice with regard to distinctive spheres of preaching. The Jerusalem pillars are to continue their focus on the Jews while Paul and Barnabas will continue largely among the Gentiles.[37] The division of labor was appropriate to the people involved, but apparently not exclusive. After all, why should it be? They had all concluded that there were not two gospels but only one. The different partners of the Jerusalem *societas* were to preach the one gospel to different audiences.

Societas partners have equal standing; in *societas* there can be no one lording it over any of the partners. Throughout Galatians 1 Paul has sought to clarify his apostolic standing. In Galatians 2:1–10 his equal status with the other apostles is confirmed once more—this time by the *societas* partnership.[38] Paul already knew himself to be fully an apostle because God had set him apart for that calling. For that reason he did not need any confirmation of it, but perhaps his readers did. Paul's opponents in Galatia have raised a question about his standing. Paul recounts his view that the Jerusalem pillars recognized him and Barnabas as equals when they joined in a *societas*. For the opponents, and those in Galatia who may be swayed by them, this resolution of the Jerusalem conference testifies to Paul's equitable partnership in the gospel with the pillars.

Paul to Gentiles
Peter " Jews

As any *societas* works itself out, different partners may contribute different things or be expected to do distinctive tasks. These differentiations do not qualify the fundamental equality of the partners. In the Jerusalem *societas*, Paul and Barnabas have one special task that they are to do along with their continued preaching to the Gentiles: they are to take up a collection for the poor of Jerusalem.[99]

The force of the agreement constituted in the Jerusalem *societas* may be tested in the Pauline corpus. Paul's letters are our best evidence of the degree of commitment and obligation. The same Paul who has boasted of preaching a gospel free of charge (1 Cor. 9:18) returns to his converts and attempts to take up a collection. One can imagine the consternation. Some misunderstand. Others oppose. Some are zealous at first but over a period of time lose their zeal. Others question Paul's motives. Despite all this, Paul persists. Remembering the poor is not an option for Paul. He is both required to do it and zealous for it. In the face of all this opposition and difficulty, Paul continues to clarify the purposes and benefits of the collection.

One further and dramatic confirmation of the force of the Jerusalem accord is Paul's final determination to deliver the collection to Jerusalem in person. For some reasons probably unknowable to us today Paul pondered having duly accredited representatives deliver the offering to Jerusalem (1 Cor. 16:3-4), but for some equally unascertainable circumstance he finally determined to deliver the collection himself—and that in the face of known danger to himself (Rom. 15:31). His willingness to face that peril is an adequate index of Paul's commitment to the collection and of the force of his agreement to it.

The Jerusalem conference, reported in Galatians 2:1-10 in such limited detail, was a watershed event in the life of early Christianity and in Paul's career. Without the consensus reached there the church seemed headed for a fundamental schism into two distinct groups, one predominantly Jewish, the other largely Gentile. The former might have remained what Christianity was in its very earliest times, a sect within Judaism. Who knows what form the Gentile group might have taken?

But, as Paul harangued the Galatians, there is only one gospel —and that single gospel produces a people of God that transcends former social and ethnic boundaries. As he reminded them, "In Christ there is neither Jew nor Greek, neither slave nor free, neither male nor female; for you are all one in Christ Jesus" (3:28). Two peoples of God cannot result from the one gospel.

In view of that concern the Jerusalem *societas* among James, Cephas, John, Barnabas, and Paul must have been a great event for Paul. It confirmed that there would be just one gospel, that all of the apostles were equally preaching it, and that each should continue to preach it in his general preconference sphere. If it was a great event for Paul, it was an even finer event in the life of the church because it was consistent with Paul's claims of the unity of diverse people in Christ. The right hand of *societas* in Jerusalem had ritualized the unity of the five partners; the collection, delivered and accepted, would symbolize the unity of all the Christians they represented.[40]

SIGNIFICANCE FOR THE EARLY CHURCH

Early in the conference account Paul lets the Galatians know that he sees broader ramifications for this meeting. When he begins to describe it he indicates why he went to Jerusalem and what he did when he met with the pillars: "I laid before them . . . the gospel which I preach among the Gentiles." And he states the reason for doing so: "lest somehow I should be running or had run in vain" (2:2). Athletic metaphors are frequent in Paul's letters.[41] Here the picture evoked is of a runner who somehow makes the race but to no avail. Victory eludes him in the contest. The curiosity of Paul's imagery is that there is a type of double jeopardy. It may be discovered that Paul has run in vain—in the past. But it may be disclosed that his present and expected running is equally in jeopardy. The outcome of the Jerusalem conference—the equitable partnership in preaching the gospel—is the

36

first necessary verdict. The church can continue in unity; the consensual partnership is established. The first hurdle is over.[42]

Involved in the Jerusalem council is not just whether Paul "had run in vain" (2:2), whether, that is, his preaching for the past decade has been voided, but also whether he "should be running . . . in vain" (2:2). In a fleeting glimpse Paul alludes to some further verdict that must be rendered. The preliminary judgment was in the hands of the Jerusalem pillars, and they have joined with Paul in full partnership. The final verdict—merely hinted in 2:2—cannot be rendered either by Paul and Barnabas or by the Jerusalem pillars. It is the Gentile hearers of the gospel who could refuse to view themselves as having a fundamental unity with other Christians. The unity of all Christians, whether Jew or Greek, of which Paul has caught the conviction and shown the Jerusalem pillars, must be demonstrated by the Gentile Christians as well. Paul puts it in terms of indebtedness (Rom. 15:27). Their means of showing forth the new unity is to generate a collection for their Jewish Christian brothers and sisters. When that offering is pulled together, delivered to the Jerusalem Christians, and accepted by them, the Gentile Christians will have recognized their debt to the Jerusalem saints (Rom. 15:27), and all will have affirmed their unity in Christ.[43] Then Paul will know himself not to have run or be running in vain.[44]

We have no account of the delivery of the collection.[45] How ironic that something so massively important in Paul's life and career drops unnoticed into the spaces between the known events of that time. We do have in Acts (22 and 23) some confirmation that Paul's trip to Jerusalem was the event that brought about the end of his career before he could undertake his projected evangelizing effort west via Rome to Spain.[46]

Paul moves from his own account of the Jerusalem conference to describe a situation in which Peter and many of the Jewish Christians in Antioch found themselves "carried away" by hypocrisy (Gal. 2:13). Even Barnabas strayed.

Galatians 2:11–21 has fueled much of the Peter-versus-Paul

mentality that burned most fully in the famed Tübingen school and that continues to glow in the hearts of many interpreters today.[47] These interpreters have reason for some thoughts of that sort. Where else can one see such forthright language of controversy as "I opposed him to his face, because he stood condemned" (2:11) or "when I saw that they were not straightforward about the truth of the gospel" (2:14)? Besides that, it is not only in this passage that Paul and Peter differ in style or point of view.

The interpreter of Galatians, however, must not lose sight of the prime controversy with which the opening chapters have been concerned. It is the Galatians who are in danger of being led astray towards what is being billed to them as a whole gospel— as distinguished from Paul's gospel which is reputed to be only partial. Against that point of view Paul has countered in a variety of ways, the latest of which is his version of the Jerusalem conference. Immediately following that account where James, Cephas, John, Barnabas, and Paul have made *societas* with each other and accepted each other as brothers in one gospel, we have a story where two of the parties of the Jerusalem contract and representatives of a third are caught in what Paul considers a compromising situation. In Antioch Peter and some other Jewish Christians were eating with their Gentile fellow Christians. But when certain "men from James" appeared Peter withdrew from table fellowship. The other Jews joined him (2:13). And even Barnabas, another of the Jerusalem partners, lost perspective and withdrew (2:13).

Paul, when relating his view of the Jerusalem conference, had expressed the concern that his "running" might have been in vain. Two gospels or two churches would be a contradiction and a betrayal of God's grace. The conference was seen by him as the first step in affirming that there was just one gospel and insuring that the people of God generated by it were one in Christ whether they be Jew or Gentile. Now he reports the Antioch confrontation not primarily as a way of deprecating Peter but as a way of telling his readers how easy it is to lose sight of the unity generated by the gospel. Even Cephas *and Barnabas* lost their focus on this newfound unity. To put it differently, Paul uses this story to make clear to the Galatian readers how easy it is to fall into the different-gospel-for-different-people mentality. From Paul's view, that leads directly to a bifurcation of the Christians into two separate camps.

It would be an interesting irony if Paul, in wishing to avoid two Christian camps on the basis of Jew and Gentile, had inadvertently created two camps along other lines, namely, Paul versus Peter. In my judgment, he does not aim for the latter, nor does he accidentally achieve it. The conference account has just shown Paul and Cephas entering a consensual partnership on equal terms with one another. Further, the Antioch situation is not just Paul versus Peter. The inclusion of Barnabas as another one of the partners who loses sight of what they have enacted sets aside the overly simple Peter-versus-Paul reading of the account.

If we ask what are the implications of this Antioch story for the Galatians, two possibilities among perhaps others suggest themselves. First, as the readers weigh whether they will go with Paul or with Paul's opponents, they ought to consider that if Paul was that firm and direct with Peter and Barnabas, his partners, what might he be with the Galatians if he were face to face with them in Galatia?

Second, from 1 Corinthians we know that Paul is capable of taking himself and Apollos as the foils by which he could point out and then mend the schismatic tendencies at work in Corinth. "I have applied all this to myself and Apollos for your benefit, brethren, that you may learn by us to live according to scripture, that none of you may be puffed up in favor of one against another" (1 Cor. 4:6). What a forceful way for Paul, in writing to the Galatians, to illustrate how difficult it is to know that in Christ "there is neither Jew nor Greek" (Gal. 3:28). Even Peter and Barnabas had difficulty living it in day-to-day events.

The Galatians are further reminded that Paul has never lost

sight of the oneness of the gospel and the unity of Jews and Gentiles in Christ. The passage that describes Peter's and Barnabas's hypocrisy (2:11 ff.) climaxes with Paul's declaration: "I have been crucified with Christ; it is no longer I who live, but Christ who lives in me; and the life I now live in the flesh I live by faith in the Son of God, who loved me and gave himself for me" (Gal. 2:20). From Paul's view all Christians share this much together; this is their starting place. From that center Christians should not go in the direction of Cephas and Barnabas.

The Roman law consensus contract of *societas* conceptualizes some of the interchanges among Christians and captures the force of the agreement that Paul understood to have taken place with the Jerusalem leaders, but the more quintessentially Pauline terminology of crucifixion with Christ and God's love shown in the death of Christ remain the central images for Paul's declaration of God's grace. These terms burst forth toward the end of Galatians 2. But just as it appears that legal terminology has completely given way to the more familiar Pauline phrases, Paul asserts: "I do not nullify the grace of God" (Gal. 2:21). Remember that the Jerusalem conference came to its *societas* conclusion when the pillars "perceived the grace that was given to me" (Gal. 2:9). With Galatians 2:21, "I do not nullify the grace of God," Paul recapitulates the decisive matter in the conference, the grace of God at work, and declares that he, Paul, does not nullify that grace. The verb translated in 2:21 as "nullify" (*atheteō*) is in fact a legal technical term meaning to "set at naught a treaty or promise," to "deal treacherously with, break faith with."[48]

Paul concludes his self-defense in Galatians with this return to legal terminology and assures the readers that he will not deal treacherously with them, that he will not break faith with them. Implicit in that may be a call for the Galatians to deal straight with him, to keep faith with him. If Paul and the Galatians together keep faith with one another and with the grace of God, then Paul will not have run in vain. In the strongest terms, Paul

40

declares his intention to do his part: "I do not nullify the grace of God."

In sum, then, the momentous event of the first hundred years of Christianity is viewed by Paul to have been a pivotal meeting. At that conference as Paul recalls it to the Galatians, all the parties recognized their true unity in Christ and in their culture found a ready way to express their formal commitment to an actual partnership in preaching the gospel. They exchanged right hands and engaged in a consensual partnership of equals around the mutual task of spreading the one gospel, one group of leaders going to the Jews, the other group going to the Gentiles.[49] Paul devoted the rest of his foreshortened career to fulfilling his commitments to the Jerusalem *societas* by preaching among Gentiles and gathering the collection.[50]

NOTES

1. Ernst Haenchen, *The Acts of the Apostles* (Philadelphia: Westminster Press, 1971), pp. 378–79, attempts to reconstruct how Luke himself may have identified the collection with the famine relief mentioned in Acts 11:29–30.

2. On the "pillars," see C. K. Barrett, "Paul and the 'Pillar' Apostles," in *Studia Paulina*, In honorem J. de Zwaan (Haarlem: Erven F. Bohn, 1953), pp. 1–19; and John H. Schütz, *Paul and the Anatomy of Apostolic Authority* (Cambridge: Cambridge University Press, 1975), pp. 140–42.

3. Cf. W. M. Ramsay, *A Historical Commentary on St. Paul's Epistle to the Galatians* (New York: G. P. Putnam's Sons, 1900), p. 296, whose reasoning strikes me as somewhat like that of Paul's Galatian opponents: "Paul, therefore, asked the advice of the three great Apostles as to the Gospel which he proposed to preach, or was preaching, among the Gentiles. It is difficult to suppose that he asked their advice about a Gospel which he had already been preaching. . . . We are therefore placed in this dilemma: either Paul consulted the Three before he promulgated his Gospel in its fully developed form or there

is no idea of 'consultation' in the verb which he here employs. The second alternative seems to me excluded."

4. On the background and function of the oath in Gal. 1:20, see my " 'Before God, I do not lie' (Gal. 1:20): Paul's Self-defence in the Light of Roman Legal Praxis," *NTS* 23 (1977): 477–82.

5. For a discussion and literature on the relation of Galatians 2 and Acts, see S. G. Wilson, *The Gentiles and the Gentile Mission in Luke-Acts* (Cambridge: Cambridge University Press, 1973), pp. 178–82. Cf. also W. G. Kümmel, *Introduction to the New Testament,* 17th ed. (Nashville: Abingdon Press, 1973), pp. 301–4. We are fortunate to have two accounts of the conference in Jerusalem, one from Paul's perspective and one from Luke's. Considerable attention has been paid to the relation of the two accounts. Indeed, which of Acts' accounts ought to be considered parallel to Gal. 2:1–10? For this study we will assume that Acts 15 and Gal. 2:1–10 are accounts of the same event even though there are significant differences in detail. Both accounts agree concerning the focal problem of the conference: Do Gentiles have to become Jews in order to be Christians? The issue is set in terms of the symbolic action of circumcision. In general both accounts agree on the resolution of that issue in the early church: Gentiles may be Christians without becoming circumcised.

6. It is not congruent with our purposes in this study to pursue more than a selected set of features in Gal. 2:1–10. Accordingly, many matters of interest must be left aside.

7. For an assessment of the Tübingen school and their stress on antipathy between Paul and Peter, see Johannes Munck, *Paul and the Salvation of Mankind* (Richmond: John Knox Press, 1959), pp. 69–86.

8. Cf. John Knox, *Chapters in a Life of Paul* (New York: Abingdon-Cokesbury Press, 1950), pp. 77–79 for the considerations in judging how many years Paul had preached by the time of the Jerusalem conference.

9. I agree with J. B. Lightfoot, *St. Paul's Epistle to the Galatians,* 2d ed. (London: Macmillan & Co., 1866), p. 103 when he translates as "the men of repute, of position" and continues "a term of honour, and conveys no shadow of depreciation" (cf. also p. 108). After all, these people are the ones who are about to be described by Paul as his equal partners. Any defamation of them would reflect on Paul himself.

10. *TDNT,* s.v. *"charis."*

11. Haenchen, *Acts of the Apostles,* p. 466, is certainly right to note

that the Jerusalem conference focuses not simply on the five named persons but has ramifications for all the Christians that each represents.

12. *TDNT*, s.v. *"dexios,"* fails to treat Gal. 2:9.

13. Hardly worthy of consideration on this point are those commentators who do not recognize in this a technical term or phrase, such as G. S. Duncan, *The Epistle of Paul to the Galatians* (New York: Harper and Brothers, 1934), p. 51. Already in 1833, L. Usteri, *Commentar über den Brief pauli an die Galater* (Zürich: Orell Fussli, 1883), p. 55, saw it as a technical phrase and cited evidence for it from Josephus, 1 Macc., and Pliny. For *dexias koinōnias* he suggested: "die rechten Hände (als Zeichen) der Gemeinschaft, freundlichen Uebereinkunft."

14. Lightfoot, *Epistle to the Galatians*, p. 110.

15. Ibid.

16. No advance is represented in the very generalizing reading offered by R. N. Longenecker, *Paul, Apostle of Liberty* (Grand Rapids: Eerdmanns, 1964), p. 222: "They pledged themselves to respect each other's commission and methods."

17. E. D. Burton, *Critical and Exegetical Commentary on the Epistle to the Galatians* (New York: Charles Scribner's Sons, 1920), p. 96.

18. Ibid.

19. For giving or keeping the right hand in contract terminology, see the following: *P.Chr.* I, 1,1,19 (3d cent. B.C.E.); *P.Oxy.* 533. 18 (2d cent. C.E.), B899. 13 (4th cent. C.E.); and B944. 11 (4th–5th cent. C.E.).

20. H. G. Liddell and R. Scott, *A Greek-English Lexicon*, 9th ed. (Oxford: Clarendon Press, 1940), p. 379.

21. Lightfoot, *Epistle to the Galatians*, p. 110.

22. Burton, *Epistle to the Galatians*, pp. 95–96: "In Greek writers . . . pledges received or given. . . . In a papyrus of the second century A.D. the expression *mē phylass]i[n sou tēn dexian,* 'not to keep your pledge' (Grenfell, Hunt, and Hogarth, *Fayum Towns and Their Papyri*, 124[13]), indicated that *dexia* had acquired the meaning 'pledge.' " For *dexias edōkan* Lightfoot, *Epistle to the Galatians*, p. 110, translates "gave pledges" and continues: "The outward gesture is lost sight of in this expression." Cf. M.-J. Lagrange, *Saint Paul Épitre aux Galates* (Paris: Gabalda, 1942), p. 38, where he says the phrase "to give the right hand" had been "longtemps metaphorique." Contra K. Grayston, "The Significance of the Word *Hand* in the New Testament," in *Mélanges Biblique en hommage au R. P. Béda Rigaux*

43

(Gembloux: Duculot, 1970), p. 484: "From what has already been said about Paul's usage, it is unlikely that he is describing a handshake with symbolic significance; he is merely using a verbal convention." Grayston's previous statements—to which the quoted sentence refers—are reasonable in their original context, namely, concerning defilement of hands. There Grayston rightly concludes: "Nowhere therefore does Paul show himself interested in the symbolic significance of hands, or in the removal of their defilement by ritual washing. Perhaps it may be said that he 'secularized' hands by abandoning the Pharisaic tradition in which he had been reared" (p. 483). But Paul was reared in the Greco-Roman world, and Pharisaic questions of defiled hands have no bearing on one's reading of a very different use of *hands* in Gal. 2:9. Grayston, like many of his predecessors, views Gal. 2:9 against the evidence from Israel's traditions and concludes that the pillars "came to terms with me and Barnabas about sharing the missionary work" (p. 485). He would have the phrase "the right hand of fellowship" disappear in his translation because of his polemic against a modern reuse of that phrase ("a poor model for Christian re-union," p. 485).

23. Lightfoot, *Epistle to the Galatians*, p. 107: "They welcomed myself and Barnabas as fellow-labourers and exchanged pledges of friendship with us. It was agreed that we should go to the Gentiles and they to the Jews." It is not Lightfoot alone who settles for generalizing interpretations of Gal. 2:9–10. Cf. A. W. Robinson, *The Epistle of Paul the Apostle to the Galatians* (London: Methuen, 1900), p. 42, "pledges of friendship and loyalty," and p. 43, "signs of mutual regard and counsels of practical charity."

24. Burton, *Epistle to the Galatians*, p. 95: "The giving of right hands is in token of a mutual compact. . . . The custom of giving the hand as a pledge of friendship or agreement existed both among the Hebrews and the Greeks, though probably derived by the Hebrews from some outside source." P. Stuhlmacher, *Das paulinische Evangelium. I. Vorgeschichte* (Göttingen: Vandenhoeck & Ruprecht, 1968), p. 98, correctly labels *dexias didonai* "Rechtsbegriff."

25. Lightfoot, *Epistle to the Galatians*, p. 110, recognizes that *koinōnias* is "not a superfluous addition," but settles for the vague term *friendship*. Cf. Burton, *Epistle to the Galatians*, p. 96, on *koinōnias* in Gal. 2:9: "implying a friendly participation in the same work (cf. Phil. 1:5) defines that which the giving of the right hands expressed and to which the givers pledged themselves." J. Y. Campbell,

Paul's View of the Jerusalem Conference

"KOINŌNIA and its Cognates in the New Testament," *JBL* 51 (1932): 373, says of *koinōnias* in Gal. 2:9: "quite definitely the sense of 'partnership,' 'going shares in an enterprise,' rather than the vaguer sense of 'fellowship.'"

26. F. Hauck, *"koinos," TDNT* 3: 789–809: *"Koinōnos* is a tt. for a business partner or associate. *Koinōnia* is used esp. of a close life partnership" (p. 798). J. H. Moulton and G. Milligan, *The Vocabulary of the Greek New Testament*, 2d ed. (London: Hodder and Stoughton, 1915), p. 351, recognize a wide range of usage for *koinōnia* and *koinōnos*. Among those, they note that both are used as contract and partnership terms. Cf. Jean Fleury, "Une Société de Fait dans l'Église Apostolique (Phil. 4:10 à 22)," in *Mélanges Philippe Meylan*, vol. 2, *Histoire du Droit* (Lausanne: Lausanne Université, 1963), p. 45: "On les retrouverait dans le grec byzantin: Théophile, dans la paraphrase des Institutes de Justinien, nous apprend que *koinōnia* désigne toute société du type contractuel." Contrast Heinrich Seesemann, *Der Begriff koinōnia im Neuen Testament* (Giessen: A. Töpelmann, 1933), p. 99: "Nirgends ist uns *koinōnia* bei Paulus als 'Gemeinschaft' im Sinn von *societas* = Genossenschaft begegnet." Seesemann denies the connection not on the basis of evidence but on the grounds of an a priori decision that *koinōnia* in Paul is a "religiöser Terminus" and therefore could not have contractual overtones as well.

27. Burton, *Epistle to the Galatians*, p. 95. Without equivocation Burton recognizes that the *koinōnia* of Gal. 2:10 "defines that compact as one of partnership," but he does not make the connection of *koinōnia* with *societas*. Arthur Lukyn Williams, *The Epistle of Paul the Apostle to the Galatians* (Cambridge: Cambridge University Press, 1936), p. 27: "'Fellowship' is here more than the spirit of fellowship and communion, almost our 'brotherliness' (Philem. 6, note), and is strictly 'partnership,' cf. Philem. 17." Williams has sensed several matters that are supported by my *societas* findings. He has caught the 'brotherly' sense of this pact, suggests 'partnership' as a translation, and sees the connection with Philem. 17.

28. Lagrange, *Épitre aux Galates*, p. 38.

29. Stuhlmacher, *Das paulinische Evangelium*, p. 100: "Es handelt sich um eine Vertragsklausel, wie das *monon hina* zeigt." Cf. Burton, *Epistle to the Galatians*, p. 99, who correctly takes v. 10 as "coordinate in construction with the preceding *hina* clause . . . and dependent on the idea of agreement implied in *dexias edōkan*. On this understanding the clause is not a request added to the agreement, but a part of the

45

agreement itself. *Monon* limits the whole clause and indicates that it contains the only qualification of the agreement already stated in general terms."

30. I hold with Haenchen and others that "Paul's formula does not give the official wording of the agreement reached in Jerusalem," that his statement is not the "official text of the protocol." See *Acts of the Apostles*, p. 465. Contra the interpretation that is reflected in Walter Schmithals, *Paul and James*, trans. C. M. Barton (London: SCM Press, 1965), p. 52: "a well-grounded conjecture that Paul in Gal. 2:7 ff. is quoting from an official record of the outcome of the discussions drawn up in Jerusalem."

31. There has been considerable debate concerning this collection, whether it should be identified with the famine relief of Acts 11:30, and whether it was a once-for-all-time event or a regular feature of Paul's relation to the Jewish Christians. Many modern interpreters see no connection with Acts 11:30 and view the collection as a singular event. I share the view of Wayne A. Meeks, ed., *The Writings of St. Paul* (New York: W. W. Norton & Co., 1972), p. 15, n. 7: the collection is "a one-time emergency fund for relief of those who were literally 'poor among the saints in Jerusalem'." But for a different voice from the past, note W. M. Ramsay, *A Historical Commentary on Paul's Epistle to the Galatians* (New York: G. P. Putnam's Sons, 1900), p. 300. And for a more recent voice in the same tradition, cf. D. R. Hall, "St. Paul and Famine Relief: A Study in Galatians 2:10," *ExpT* 82 (1971): 309–11. The collection has been the subject of several monographs, including: Dieter Georgi, *Die Geschichte der Kollekte des Paulus für Jerusalem* (Hamburg: Bergstedt, 1965), and Keith F. Nickle, *The Collection: A Study in Paul's Strategy* (Naperville: A. R. Allenson, 1966).

32. Cf. L. E. Keck, "The Poor among the Saints in the New Testament," *ZNW* 56 (1965): 100–129. On the basis of a fresh examination of the evidence, Keck rejects K. Holl's ("Der Kirchenbegriff des Paulus in seinem Verhältnis zu dem der Urgemeinde," in *Gesammelte Aufsätze* [Tübingen: J. C. B. Mohr, 1928], 2: 44–67, cf. esp. 59 ff.) claim that "the poor" is a designation for all Christians or the church. Keck properly sees it as a particular reference to the indigent members of the church of Jerusalem. So also, Hans Conzelmann, *1 Corinthians* (Philadelphia: Fortress Press, 1975), p. 295, and Ragnar Bring, *Commentary on Galatians*, trans. E. Wahlstrom (Philadelphia: Muhlenberg Press, 1961), p. 76. For further treatments of the question of poverty in the early church, see H. Bolkestein, *Wohltätigkeit und*

Armenplflege im vorchristlichen Altertum (Utrecht: A. Oosthoek, 1939; reprint ed., Groningen, 1967), and Martin Hengel, *Property and Riches in the Early Church* (Philadelphia: Fortress Press, 1974). Note Hengel's bibliography, pp. 89–92. See *TDNT*, s.v. *"ptōchos."*

33. I agree with Schmithals, *Paul and James,* p. 79, against K. Holl, "Der Kirchenbegriff," that the collection was not a response to a legal tax or levy imposed on the Gentile Christians by the Jerusalem church. That it does have legal overtones for Paul, I could not deny, however. In that regard Schmithals may be a bit sweeping when he says, "It is certain that Paul did not understand this obligation to be a legal one, whatever its intention" (p. 79). In any case, Schmithals is right that the "legal sovereignty" of the Jerusalem church is not involved.

34. H. W. Bartsch, ". . . wenn ich ihnen dies Frucht versiegelt habe. Röm 15:28. Ein Beitrag zum Verständnis der paulinischen Mission," *ZNW* 63 (1972): 95–107, takes *karpos* in Rom. 15:28 to refer not to the collection but to the Macedonians and the Achaeans whom Paul converted. By delivering the collection, Paul seals the givers as fruit of the Jerusalem community.

35. Paul's collection should not be confused with the famine relief mentioned in Acts 11:28 ff. Also rejecting the identification of Gal. 2:10 and Acts 11:30 are H. N. Ridderbos, *The Epistle of Paul to the Churches of Galatia* (Grand Rapids: Eerdmanns, 1953), pp. 31–35, and J. A. Allan, *The Epistle of Paul the Apostle to the Galatians* (London: SCM Press, 1954), pp. 23–26.

36. *TDNT*, s.v. *"eleutheros."* Cf. V. P. Furnish, *Theology and Ethics in Paul* (Nashville: Abingdon Press, 1968), pp. 176–81.

37. Cf. Haenchen's weighing of this distinction, *Acts of the Apostles*, pp. 466–68. Posing rigid alternatives may distort one's answers. A classic example is Schmithals, *Paul and James,* p. 46: "Paul relinquished the mission to the Jews, Peter that to the Gentiles." Peter and Paul are understood by Schmithals to have run separate but parallel Jewish and Gentile missions. We have no reason to suppose rigidly separate spheres of operation. Paul's own letters make clear that such was not the case. Cephas, "the brothers of the Lord," and other apostles travel about, preaching the gospel. The Corinthians know of that practice. In fact, the Corinthians probably supported some of those apostles—and maybe even their wives too—on junkets into Gentile quarters (1 Cor. 9:5). Paul tells, or reminds, the Galatians that some representatives of James showed up in Antioch (Gal. 2:12). And someone other than Paul established the church in Rome. So Paul's letters show that there never was an absolute distinction of spheres of

operation. The Jerusalem *societas* therefore confirmed the division of labor that had come to prevail prior to the conference.

38. We can now see the precise grounds on which Haenchen, *Acts of the Apostles,* p. 467, may say the following: "As Paul formulates the result, it makes him (and Barnabas) of equal rank and stature with the 'pillars' they confront—and this was important for Paul in this context. Mere permission for a Gentile mission apart from the law would have made Jerusalem appear still the superior authority, which had simply thought fit to make a gracious concession."

39. F. F. Bruce, *1 and 2 Corinthians* (London: Oliphants, 1971), p. 158, says Gal. 2:10 "perhaps amounted to a request" to continue what they had begun in famine relief (Acts 11:30). Apart from the mistaken identification of the collection with the Acts famine relief, Bruce waters down the force of the agreement when he treats the offering as a request. The *societas* among the pillars and Paul and Barnabas included that task as a part of the initial agreement.

40. Stuhlmacher, *Das paulinische Evangelium,* p. 98, and Haenchen, *Acts of the Apostles,* p. 466 both rightly stress this representative role played by all five parties to the Jerusalem conference.

41. Victor C. Pfitzner, *Paul and the Agon Motif* (Leiden: E. J. Brill, 1967), p. 100: "In each case [Gal. 2:2; Phil. 2:16; and 1 Cor. 9:26 ff.] Paul appears as the *agōnistēs* of the Gospel, and in each case the thought of the goal is uppermost in his mind, together with the thought of his possible failure to reach the goal."

42. H. J. Schoeps, *Paul: The Theology of the Apostle in Light of Jewish Religious History* (Philadelphia: Westminster Press, 1961), p. 68: "The right hand of fellowship (Gal. 2:9), with which the *styloi* admit Paul to the apostolic circle, signifies their honest recognition (v. 7) of the Pauline mission to the Gentiles, their acceptance of the fact that Paul was entrusted with the gospel to the Gentiles, just as Peter was entrusted with its preaching to the circumcision. It meant the two men were in co-operation rather than in conflict." Pfitzner, *The Agon Motif,* pp. 101–2: "The purpose of his journey is to establish and preserve the unity of this one Gospel and the one Church composed of Jews and Gentiles, lest a schism should occur and the fruits of his labour be destroyed by the clash between two conflicting gospels." The positive response of the pillars is necessary for Paul but only a first step towards the preservation of the unity of the gospel and the church.

43. Paul S. Minear, *The Obedience of Faith* (London: SCM Press,

1971), p. 5: "In some way the preservation of unity between Jewish and Gentile churches depended upon the delivery of the aid."

44. Haenchen, *Acts of the Apostles*, p. 613: "But if James and the elders refused the Pauline collection, then the connection between the Pauline Gentile Church and the Church of Jerusalem would be severed. . . . 'He would run in vain.'"

45. Haenchen, *Acts of the Apostles*, p. 613: "Even in [Acts] 24:17 the word 'collection' does not occur; no reader who knew only Acts but not the Pauline epistles could deduce from this verse the great Pauline work of the collection. This silence of Luke's is extremely surprising."

46. Minear, *Obedience of Faith*, p. 4: "His life was the price he finally paid for fulfilling his promise to Peter and James." And to John!

47. Munck, *Paul and the Salvation*, pp. 69–86.

48. Henry G. Liddell and Robert Scott, eds., *Greek-English Lexicon*, 9th ed. (Oxford: Oxford University Press, 1940), p. 31. Cf. F. Wilbur Gingrich and Frederick W. Danker, eds., *A Greek-English Lexicon of the New Testament*, 2d ed. rev. (Grand Rapids: Zondervan Publishing House, 1979), p. 21, and J. H. Moulton and G. Milligan, *The Vocabulary of the Greek Testament*, 2d ed. (London: Hodder and Stoughton, 1915), p. 12.

49. Grayston, "*Hand* in the New Testament," p. 485: "It should also be said that every example of this symbolism [of giving the right hand] describes an agreement made entirely on the human level. Nowhere does it imply that God is active in the agreement; it is always a compact on human terms. Even the apostolic compact arose from recognizing what God had already done—which is perhaps different from the laying on of hands in which God himself is supposed to act." As this chapter shows, matters sacred and profane in Paul are not as neat and discrete as Grayston would have us believe.

50. I have stressed throughout this chapter that in the Galatians account, we have access to Paul's perception of the Jerusalem conference, its significance and its force. I have noted that Acts does not portray the conference as concluding in a *societas;* it is Paul who understood the giving of the right hands and the joint commitment to preaching the gospel in that way. I want now to share an observation that has haunted me but that probably cannot be advanced as more than speculation. Is the following scenario possible on the basis of the Pauline evidence and on the basis that even in situations and occasions of great importance different people can understand the significance of the occasion in strikingly different ways? The five principals

did come to see that they were preaching the one gospel; the three Jerusalem pillars did offer the right hand to Paul and Barnabas; all five did agree to preach the gospel along the preconference pattern. But is it possible that the three Jerusalem pillars, steeped in Judaism, understood the symbolism and force of that agreement in a fundamentally different way from Paul? When they gave the right hand were they symbolizing agreement along the Burton lines of the superiors acknowledging the subordinates? That would be fully in line with Jewish tradition for the giving of the right hand. And Paul—and perhaps Barnabas—being familiar with Roman law understood it as the forming of a partnership of equals, a consensual *societas*. This reading suggests that the different parties may have had quite different understandings of the significance of the giving of the right hands. All five would have affirmed a certain unity, but the precise terms and force of the agreement would have been understood in radically different ways. The proclaimers of one gospel met in Jerusalem, but it is possible that two different cultures, two worlds, clashed in their perceptions of the way they ritualized their unity.

4 *Excellent*

Societas Christi with the Philippians

Long an important city in the hellenistic world—as its name suggests—Philippi was an official Roman colony in Paul's time.[1] As such, Philippi enjoyed certain privileges and responsibilities in the empire. In particular its status as a colony meant that the same legal structures applicable in Rome were guaranteed to the citizens of Philippi. Sometime within a hundred years before Paul journeyed into Philippi, Latin became the official language of the city and even filtered out into the countryside as well.[2] The use of Greek persisted, however.[3] Romans and Greeks inhabited the city together.[4] It is with the Christians in this city, Philippi, that Paul most clearly and consistently claims that he has *societas*, the Roman legal contract of consensual partnership.[5]

We have seen that Paul viewed his newfound unity with the pillars at the Jerusalem conference via the norms and patterns of the consensual *societas*. What we encounter in his Letter to the Philippians is Paul's application of this same contractual partnership to refer now to his relationship to the Christians in Philippi. Paul and they have joined together in a consensual partnership in Christ for preaching the gospel. They have become a *societas Christi*. There are three sets of data in the extant Philippians Letter that establish the presence of this unusual conception.[6] They are: (1) the receipt Paul writes for the gift or payment that he has received via Epaphroditus, (2) the appearance of *koinōnia* used in the sense of partnership known in *societas*, and (3) the prominent use of the terminology of *societas*.

51

*Jesyts n
vrf 4:10.20*

I   PAUL'S RECEIPT TO THE PHILIPPIANS 4:10.20

It must be recalled that in *societas* the expenses incurred by one of the partners in his work on behalf of the partnership are to be reimbursed by the remaining partners.[7] One of the reasons Paul writes to the Philippians is to acknowledge the Philippian support sent by way of Epaphroditus. The first mention of the assistance appears in 2:25 ff. where Paul tells the Philippians that he is sending Epaphroditus back home to them. Epaphroditus, who nearly died "to complete your service to me" (2:27,30), is described by Paul from two perspectives. To Paul Epaphroditus is "brother," "fellow worker," and "fellow soldier"; to the Philippians he is "your delegated representative [*apostolos*] and minister to my need." Paul encourages the Philippians to accept this man back with appropriate joy and honor because he has completed his task and experienced such a close scrape with death.

But it is not until 4:10–20, the curious passage that concludes the canonical letter, that the Philippian support of Paul is treated in detail. When viewed against the background provided by the remaining Pauline corpus it is a curious passage in at least two ways. First, it shows Paul taking support from one of the churches that he has established. That is singular enough, but, even more strikingly, this is not the first time Paul has accepted Philippian support. In fact, Paul states this most recent aid was the third time for them to help him: "Even in Thessalonica you sent me help once and again" (4:16). The Corinthians know that Paul's "needs were supplied by the brethren who came from Macedonia" (2 Cor. 11:9) and apparently have raised the complaint against Paul that while he accepts support from other Christian churches he will accept none from them. In the course of dealing with that complaint, Paul confirms that he has received support from the Macedonians (2 Cor. 11:9), probably the Philippians, and corroborates the picture that develops in the letter that bears their name.

Second, the passage is somewhat unusual because of the frequency of commercial technical terms.[8] From many of Paul's letters we know that he used technical terms of law and commerce, but the frequency of them in Philippians 4:10–20 is unparalleled. Furthermore, some of these terms are *hapax legomena* in the Pauline corpus although they are common in extant commercial documents.

In Philippians 4:10–20 the crucial verse is: "I have received full payment, and more; I am filled, having received from Epaphroditus the gifts you sent, a fragrant offering, a sacrifice acceptable and pleasing to God" (4:18). In this sentence Paul writes what amounts to a formal receipt, using the technical commercial term *apechō*, "I have received," so common in papyri receipts.[9] As Beare has put it, *apechō* in the documents from the turn of the eras is "a word as unmistakable as the mark of a rubber stamp on a bill, PAID. This alone would be enough to tell us that we are reading Paul's receipt for the gifts from Philippi."[10]

That this transaction—Paul's acceptance of Philippian support and his written acknowledgement of it—is possible with *societas,* we know from our earlier delineation of the characteristics of *societas.* Partners are due reimbursement for their work in behalf of the partnership.[11] Paul preaches the gospel beyond Macedonia as the representative of the Philippians, and they have a long-standing practice of supporting him in this effort on their behalf. The Philippian support of Paul is linked with *societas:* "You Philippians yourselves know that in the beginning of the gospel, when I left Macedonia, no church entered into partnership [*ekoinōnēsen*] with me in giving and receiving except you only" (4:15).

The Philippians joined Paul in a partnership involving giving and receiving, *eis logon doseōs kai lēmpseōs. Eis logon* is a frequent commercial technical phrase meaning "in settlement of an account."[12] Philippians 4:10–20 is both an expression of appreciation to the Philippians for their most recent support and at the same time is a receipt, a current reckoning of their ongoing account with Paul.

Paul refers to the latest Philippian support as *to doma* (4:17), a term that may quite readily be translated as "gift." Indeed, the RSV so translates it: "Not that I seek the gift; but I seek the fruit which increases to your credit" (4:17). But *to doma* can equally well be translated "payment."[13] Then notice how it reads: "It is not the payment that I seek; rather I seek the fruit. . . . I have received full payment and even more" (4:17–18). It would probably be wrong, however, to reduce the ambivalence of *to doma* by insisting that one be chosen over the other. Such a reduction would mean that *societas* would be either simply a commercial metaphor or quite distinctly a metaphor of Christian community. Secular and sacred are not so neatly distinct in Paul's letters. Paul's *societas* with the Philippians is both concrete relationship and obligation and at the same time points beyond itself to God's purposes. Because *societas Christi* is never just one commercial partnership among others, it is possible to see that for Paul and the Philippians *to doma* is both gift and payment.

It is also worth noting that the term *chreia* (2:25 and 4:16, 19) is regularly translated by the RSV as "need." It is this *chreia* to which the Philippians responded by *to doma*, the gift-payment. But *chreia* may also mean "request."[14] The usual reading of these appearances of *chreia* in Philippians supposes that somehow the Philippians learned of Paul's need for aid or support and responded to it at their first opportunity. Accordingly, the RSV translates 2:25 "Epaphroditus . . . your messenger and minister to my need," 4:16 "you sent me help [*eis tēn chreian moi epempsate*] once and again," and 4:19 "my God will supply every need of yours." This interpretive choice of "need" over "request" is reinforced by what I would dub corpus harmonization, where Paul's otherwise prevalent claim of financial independence is read into Philippians, a letter that resists it consistently and directly. In this instance of corpus harmonization the peculiarities of the Philippian correspondence tend to be sacrificed to a construct that admittedly is present in some of the other letters.[15]

Why would it not be possible to translate each occurrence of *chreia* in Philippians equally well as "need" or "request"? For a group of Christians so generally in sympathy with Paul as the Philippians, any expression of "need" was likely to have the force of "request." In Paul's relations with the Philippians the two possible meanings probably coalesce. Interpreters of *chreia* in Philippians should probably leave operative the full range of meaning, need-request. Surely there is no problem with that reading of 4:19, "And my God will supply every need-request of yours according to his riches." For many interpreters, however, the problem will come in the other appearances of *chreia*: "Epaphroditus . . . your messenger and minister to my need-request" (2:25) and "in Thessalonica you sent [*to doma*, understood] to me at my need-request once and again." How can the Paul who so rigorously refused financial support from the Corinthians (1 Cor. 9:18; 2 Cor. 11:7–11) not only have accepted it from the Philippians but also have requested it from them? If *chreia* is translated as request, it certainly makes plausible reading out of 4:10: "I rejoice in the Lord that now at length you have revived your concern for me; you were indeed concerned for me, but you had no opportunity." Paul has communicated a need-request for support. There has been a delay in the response from the Philippians. Was the delay because they lacked concern for Paul? No, it was the result of lack of opportunity. When the opportunity came the Philippians sent Paul the payment-gift he had requested. Corpus harmonization levels out the interpretation of Paul. Interpreters of Paul must allow for singular, unique relationships between Paul and his different churches, especially when Paul says directly that a given relationship is unique (4:15). Paul was not always the same thing to all his churches. Neither were all his churches the same to him in all particulars.

The last section of the Letter to the Philippians (4:10–20) is a formal receipt tendered by Paul to the Philippian Christians for their gift-payment in response to his need-request.[16] On one level it is a commonplace commercial transaction between partners. Paul in no way demeans that. But neither does he content himself to view it *simply* as one more commercial partnership transaction. He transposes the transaction onto another level, into a larger vista, where it can now be seen in the context of Paul's own conduct and God's purposes in Christ. Let us examine this transposition in 4:10–20.

Philippians 4:10–20 opens with Paul's rejoicing in the Lord that the Philippians have at last experienced a rebirth of their concern for him. Indeed, they were concerned, but they had not found a fitting occasion until recently. He then (4:11) assures them that he is not complaining of want or lack of anything. In the great Cynic-Stoic tradition, he declares that he has learned how to deal with the extreme circumstances that life can present to him.[17] He has learned *autarkeia*, self-control. He can flow with the tide. When there is abundance, he can enjoy it. When there is nothing, he can take that too. Those parameters of life's possibilities do not shatter his contentment or self-control, but for a specifically Christian reason: Paul recognizes that the strength to abide the vagaries of life comes not from some inner discipline but from "him who strengthens me" (4:13). There he parts company with the Cynic-Stoic tradition.[18]

As in chapter 2 Paul's imprisonment caused him to reflect on the way in which life and death are relativized, so also in chapter 4 Paul declares that plenty and need are relative matters. The reason? It is the same Lord who sustains him in either extreme. Paul's argument moves along: nevertheless (*plēn*, v. 14) it was good of the Philippians to share (*sugkoinōnēsantes*) Paul's sufferings and to come to his aid in a time of need-request.

Then, in verses 15–16, he views their recent gift-payment in the context of their partnership (*societas*) characterized by giving and receiving from the very start. In that sense it is appropriate, and he writes them a receipt in verse 18, "I have received full payment," but not before he reminds them that the gift-payment pales in importance in face of the larger purposes that he is about. "Not that I seek the gift-payment; but I seek the fruit which increases to your credit" (4:17). Paul's personal need or

56

lack of need, Paul's enduring partnership with the Philippians, Paul's repeated acceptances of support from them—all these seem relatively less important in view of the larger purposes in which Paul and the Philippians are jointly engaged. What is (another) gift or payment? What is really important is the fruit that chalks up credit on a more important ledger. The introduction of the notion "fruit" may sound like the mixing of metaphors of which Paul is so capable, but the term *fruit* is sometimes used in commercial parlance of the times to mean profit.[19]

By analogy from his own *societas* with the Philippians, characterized in 4:15 as one of balancing accounts (*eis logon*) by giving and receiving,[20] Paul suggests that what matters more than their own personal bookkeeping[21] in the partnership is that the Philippians keep bearing fruit for their more important account (v. 17, *eis logon humōn*).[22] Though not explicitly identified in 4:17, that more important account is understood to be with God—as becomes clear in 4:18–19.

With 4:18 Paul stamps *Paid* on the written receipt of this mundane transaction and in a retrospective glance toward his claims in 4:11–13, where he said he could live in want or in plenty, concludes that the receipt of their support moves him from the extreme of want to the extreme of plenty. Philippians 4:18 could be translated: "I have received full payment and I (now therefore) abound."

The commercial terminology of bookkeeping within a partnership has been useful to Paul in expressing the relation of the partners to one another. In 4:17 the terminology has even been pushed to help express their common involvement in a larger purpose, an account that is reckoned beyond the day-to-day transactions of commerce. But the commercial terms do not suffice to express the larger significance of the Philippians' support of Paul. As 4:18 progresses, the commercial expressions fade and Paul transposes his evaluation of the Philippian gift into more traditional terms of sacrifice and offering.[23]

Accordingly, the gifts brought from Philippi by Epaphroditus are not merely presented to Paul; they are also "a fragrant offering, a sacrifice acceptable and pleasing to God" (4:19). As the terminology of bookkeeping moved from an account among the Philippians and Paul to an account established by the Philippians before God, so Paul enlarges the gift-payment idea into talk about offering and sacrifice before God.

The whole issue of gift-payment was introduced by Paul's request-need (*chreia*). Appropriately, the letter moves full circle to a final reference to need-request (*chreia*), but this time it is the Philippians' needs or requests. Just as the Philippians responded to Paul's need, Paul declares "my God will supply every need-request of yours according to his riches in glory in Christ Jesus" (4:19). A mundane contractual performance by the Philippians towards Paul mirrors the wealth of God's care for every need-request of his faithful. The grandeur of this vision moves Paul to conclude: "To our God and Father be glory for ever and ever" (4:20).

The *societas* relationship between Paul and the Philippians was noticed earlier by Jean Fleury of the Lausanne law faculty. Fleury and I agree that consensual *societas* is at stake, although he inclines, on the basis of Acts 16:20–40 and the mention of Lydia, to think that the *societas* partnership is established with Lydia and whatever others may be in her trade. According to Fleury, Paul has been in a moneymaking enterprise with Lydia and associates. They have split up the profits on previous occasions (4:16) and now, with this last amount, Paul finds that he has more than he needs (*perisseuō*, 4:17). Therefore Paul terminates his business relationship with Lydia and associates.[25] From this time on Paul kept to the pattern that we see in Acts and that is found in the Corinthian correspondence: Paul insisted on working to support himself and accepted no support from any of his churches. So Fleury.

I agree with him that Paul had a *societas* with the Philippian Christians, but not with just some of them. Whereas Fleury holds that Paul terminated the *societas* when he wrote *apechō de panta*,

I maintain that Paul thereby receipts their latest contribution to his activities in behalf of the *societas.*[26] It is not a splitting of profits from some business enterprise but a sharing of the costs of Paul's representing the Philippians in his preaching of the gospel. Fleury's interpretation would eliminate any discrepancy in Paul's financial dealings with his different churches. Fleury has Paul terminate his acceptance of support from the Philippians, and a consistent, self-supporting Paul results.

Though corpus harmonization may have helped Fleury interpret *apechō de panta* as terminating *societas* and not just receipting the latest payment-gift so that Paul moves into a self-supporting pattern entirely, the chief problems with Fleury's insistence that Paul ended *societas* lie within Philippians itself. As we shall see shortly, the *societas* terminology is not at all restricted to 4:10–20, the passage that has thus far been under consideration in this section of our study. Furthermore, at no point is there any indication that the *societas* material is addressed to any fragment of the readership in the church at Philippi. On the contrary, the Letter opens, in its salutation, to "all the saints . . . at Philippi," and Paul goes on a few verses later to say that he is "thankful for your partnership [*koinōnia*] in the gospel from the first day until now" (1:15).

Finally, Fleury's interpretation of 4:18 as Paul's termination of *societas* is flawed because Fleury fails to note the flow of 4:10–20 itself. Paul opens the passage rejoicing that the Philippians have found occasion to meet his needs. *Then* Paul sets his need or request in the context of life's extremes, abundance and want. Paul says he can take either extreme because of the one who strengthens him. Twice in one verse Paul uses the verb *perisseuein*, "to have plenty" (4:12), as a way of delineating the one extreme in which life may appear. Paul has been in great need. The Philippians have responded generously. Paul writes a receipt: "I have received full payment [*apechō de panta*]" and, in an *inclusio* back to 4:12, adds *kai perisseuō*, "and I abound."[27] I have plenty. Paul is not terminating *societas*. He is saying that the Philippian gift-payment has been received and has transported him from one extreme, want, to the other, plenty. But the reader already knows that Paul can take it either way, whether in want or in plenty, because of the one who strengthens him. As he has taken want, now he takes plenty. Accordingly, he provides a receipt for their most recent support and reminds them that its significance is not merely some contractual responsibility. Neither is the central concern Paul's situation of need or plenty. What matters is their account with God, who will answer their needs as they have responded to Paul's. So Fleury is right when he sees that Paul has established consensual *societas* with the Philippians, but he is wide of the mark when he maintains that it is simply commercial, engages just a few of the Philippians, and is terminated by Paul. Let us turn now to examine the further evidence that Paul had established a *societas* with the Philippian Christians.

KOINŌNIA AS A TECHNICAL TERM FOR SOCIETAS IN PHILIPPIANS

As we have already seen in connection with the right hand of *koinōnia* that concluded the Jerusalem conference, *koinōnia* may function several different ways in the Pauline letters, but when certain associated terminology is present *koinōnia* can be used by Paul to refer to the consensual partnership that in Roman law came to be known as *societas*.[28] In Philippians the term *koinōnia* appears in the section 4:10–20 that we have seen in so many other ways to reflect *societas*. It appears incidentally in 4:14 when Paul says, "Yet it was kind of you to share [*sugkoinōnēsantes*] my trouble," and if the term is to be taken as a reference to *societas* it means that the Philippians' partnership with Paul extends even to their sharing his tribulation with him. Though this reference may be ambiguous the one in the next verse is unmistakable, as we have seen: "No church entered into partnership [*oudemia moi ekklēsia ekoinōnēsen*] with me in giving and receiving except you only" (4:15). The commercial technical terms associ-

ated with *koinōnia* there leave it unmistakable that the partnership is *societas*.

That usage of *koinōnia* is mirrored in the thanksgiving which
opens the Letter to the Philippians: "I thank my God in all my
remembrance of you . . . thankful for your partnership in the
gospel [*epi tē koinōnia humōn eis to euaggelion*] from the first
day until now" (1:3, 5).[29] "From the first day until now" at the
beginning of the canonical letter is paralleled by the statement at
the end of the letter, "in the beginning of the gospel." "And you
Philippians yourselves know that in the beginning of the gospel,
when I left Macedonia, no church entered into partnership with
me . . . except you only" (4:15).

We can therefore reconstruct some details out of the time Paul
first preached the gospel in Philippi. Paul, himself a Roman
citizen, entered the Roman colony of Philippi, where the law and
institutions of Rome were replicated, and began to preach his
gospel. The Philippians recognized their new situation in Christ
and found themselves brought into a new association on a new
basis. *Koinōnia* rang in their ears, not just of a fellowship of the
faithful but as a partnership of the faithful. The overtones of
societas helped them understand their new situation in Christ.
They joined with Paul as equal partners in living and preaching
the gospel.[30] Paul became their representative, and periodically
they sent him support for his evangelistic endeavors in their behalf.

In Philippians there is a curious feature that lends corroboration
to this unusual relationship Paul had with the Philippians. The
Philippians are Paul's brothers and sisters in Christ. In their relationship they are equal partners. Now the curious feature: in
most of the salutations that open the letters, Paul identifies himself as apostle. So Romans, the Corinthian letters, and Galatians;
Ephesians and Colossians do also. Of the unquestioned letters,
only Philippians, 1 Thessalonians, and Philemon do not so desig-
nate him. What is to be made of 1 Thessalonians in this regard
is unclear, but the other two happen to be *societas* letters. In fact,

even more strikingly, the only appearance of the term *apostle* in the entire letter to the Philippians is in 2:25 and refers not to Paul but to Epaphroditus: "I have thought it necessary to send to you Epaphroditus my brother and fellow worker and fellow soldier, and your messenger [the word is *apostolos*] and minister to my need." Paul does not see any threat to his authority and therefore to his gospel in Philippi, so he does not have to secure it by using the title "apostle" for himself. His relationship with the Philippians is so stable—and has been right along—that he has no need to refer to himself in a way that sets him apart. He is a partner with them. They are therefore his fellow workers, fellow soldiers, his brothers and sisters. Of all the Pauline churches this one seems to have given Paul the least grief and the greatest joy. The Philippians have been his partners from the very beginning and have never wavered from it.[31] To be sure, there are some sections of the letter that remind the Philippians of the implications of their partnership and urge them to live up to them. And to those we now turn as we present the final portion of our evidence for *societas Christi* among Paul and the Philippian Christians.

3. SOCIETAS PARTNERS ARE "OF THE SAME MIND"

The final indicator that Paul and the Philippians understand themselves to be partners in a *societas Christi* is found in the letter's use of *phronein*, "to think," "to set one's mind on," "to be minded or disposed."[32] In all the other undisputed Pauline letters *phronein* occurs eleven times; in Philippians alone it appears ten times. It will be recalled that Gaius, in his codification of the Roman legal traditions, shows that consensual *societas* is operative as long as the partners are *in eodem sensu*, as long as they are "of the same mind" about the centrality of the purpose around which the partnership was formed in the first place. As long as all the partners are disposed in the same way, the contract continues. *Societas* terminates with the loss of unanimity, single-mindedness, among the partners.

The Philippians are fully aware of the significance of the phrase *to auto phronein*, "to have the same mind." Paul hardly has to explain it to them. When he deals with the problem of Euodia and Syntyche (4:2–3), he does not have to tell the Philippians what difficulty these two women are having. Even more importantly, Paul can exhort the two people individually *to auto phronein*, and they are expected to understand it. We interpreters, now some nineteen centuries later, can understand it because enough clues have surfaced so that we can tell that when he was with the Philippians Paul found himself understanding with them that they were bound into a partnership, a *societas* in Christ. Euodia and Syntyche are to regain their focus on the ground of their unity. What bound Euodia and Syntyche together in the first place was their shared, common commitment to the same goal. Other matters, for example, what the two women may think of each other as individuals, do not play an important role. Their unity is not in their personal like for one another or opinions about each other. Rather their bond is in Christ.

Two other occurrences of *phronein* help us understand more precisely how the *to auto phronein* is connected to Christ, that is, how the *societas* relates to Christ. Fortunately they appear together in the rather complex rhetorical construction that opens Philippians 2 and leads into the well-known hymn of Christ. Our primary interest lies not with the hymn itself but with the five verses opening the chapter and leading into the hymn, since it is those verses that contain the double use of *phronein*.

The structure of Philippians 2:1–5 is instructive. The passage opens with four *ei* (if)-clauses, in paratactic relationship. These clauses lead up to the main verb, *plērōsate*, "fill out," "complete." Paul says if these four things are present, complete my joy. The four if-clauses are not to be read as discrete matters, each to be checked out independently of one another. Rather they are facets one of another. If the one is present, the likelihood is that the others are also. This pattern of piling up of phrases is not unknown in Paul and should prepare the reader for the appearance of further overlapping of phrases coming up in the next few verses. Once Paul declares "complete my joy" (2:2a) the structure of the passage flows rather freely in positives and negatives towards the hymn in 2:6 ff.

Complete my joy (2:2a)

POSITIVES, A	NEGATIVES, B
by being *of the same mind,* having the same love, being in full accord and *of one mind.* (2:2b, A¹)	
	Do nothing from selfishness or conceit, (2:3a, B¹)
but in humility count others better than yourselves. (2:3b, A²)	
	Let each of you look not only to his own interests, (2:4a, B²)
but also to the interests of others. (2:4b, A³)	
Have this mind among yourselves, (2:5a)	

Which you have in Christ Jesus (2:5b), who . . .

The structure proceeds as follows: If these four things (2:1) are present, complete my joy (2:2a) by A¹, not B¹, but A², not B², but A³ (correctio). Then, with a recapitulation of the primary phrase of A¹ (*touto phroneite en humin,* "have this mind among yourselves"), Paul introduces the hymn of Christ (2:6–11).

As the four *ei* (if)-clauses that open up 2:1 are to be understood as complementary, so also the different words and phrases of A¹ (2:2) are to be understood as closely interrelated and intertwined.[35] "Having the same love" is not distinct from "being of the same mind." On the contrary, they are epexegetical of one another. In verse 2 the piling up of phrases continues. To have the same mind is to have the same love, is to be in full accord (*sumpsychoi*). This reading is confirmed when at the end of verse

2 (A¹ in the chart above) Paul returns to the same root word (*phronountes*) with which he opened the verse and repeats it, with *hen,* "one," rather than *auto,* "same," probably for rhetorical variation.[36]

From *societas* we know that to be of the same mind is to maintain the commitment to the goal about which *societas* was formed. The occurrence of the *societas* terminology in 2:2 shows Paul elaborating on what it means to have the same mind in Christ. As is so typical for Paul, the motifs and terms that he quite freely uses to express what God has done in Christ are always turned and modified to his own purposes. "Being of the same mind" is now explained by its epexegetical position with the next phrase, "having the same love." Immediately the matter is transferred from some simply functional notion of contractual obligation into the richness of the community relation that Paul expresses by his understanding of love.

Paul does not stop there. He fills in the picture even more fully. Being "of the same mind" is related to having "the same love" as both are related to being "in full accord" (*sumpsychoi*). The first Pauline elaboration of *to auto phronein* is completed with the recapitulation of the phrase, this time cast in slightly different form, *to hen phronountes* (2:2).

The content thus expressed for *to auto phronein* is expanded by the introduction of the rhetorical device *correctio,* in this instance taking the form of A, not B, but A. Actually, since 2:3c is not simply a restatement of 2:2 but an expansion of it, the form might better be represented as A¹ (2:2), not B¹ (2:3a–b), but A² (2:3c). Thus in a negative fashion 2:3a–b, "do nothing from selfishness or conceit," defines selfishness and conceit as inappropriate or counter to *to auto phronein,* being "of the same mind." From what we know of *societas,* both these postures would run counter to the unity and reciprocity, even brotherhood, that we know to be basic to *societas.* From what we know about Paul, both selfishness and conceit destroy or erode community among believers. Partisanship and conceit are fundamentally alien to *societas.*

The *correctio* returns in 2:3c to a positive restatement of what is involved in being of the same mind: "In humility count others better than yourselves." Humility, *tapeinophrosunē*, is basic to *societas*. Humility, not partisanship or conceit, contributes to or makes possible being of the same mind.

In 2:4 the structure advances even further to suggest that each person look not (the RSV adds *only*) to his own interests, but especially (*kai*) to the interests of others. Self-seeking or looking to satisfy one's own needs is ruled out of order. A countersuggestion is put in its place: seek the things that serve others. The *societas* that Paul sees at work in Philippi maintains its unity, its love, by avoiding selfishness and conceit. This *societas* works as the individuals, in humility, reckon others better than themselves, as the individuals give up their own self-seeking and concern themselves for the needs of others in the community of believers.

This structure in 2:1–4 serves to elaborate in more typically Pauline terms what is involved in *to auto phronein*. In 2:5 the construction is rounded out as Paul picks up the theme of *phronein* again and leads into the hymn of Christ. "Have this mind among yourselves, which you have in Christ Jesus, who . . ." [37]

Prior to the hymn in 2:6 ff., the reader encounters a veritable handbook (2:1–5) sketching out what is appropriate to *societas* and what is inappropriate to it. That the material in these verses is so epigrammatic and laconic suggests that Paul is not going over this matter with the Philippians for the first time in the letter. On the contrary, they all know and subscribe to this and have done so from the very beginning (1:5). That is how in so few words Paul (1) can elicit their memory of what it means to live together in the same mind and (2) can entreat Euodia and Syntyche to be *to auto phronein*.

One factor, however, remains to be treated in this connection. The hymn of Christ is introduced by the phrase: "Have this mind among yourselves, which you have in Christ Jesus" (2:5). Having the same mind is not simply some agreement reached among indi-

viduals. Rather its referent is beyond itself. From Paul's standpoint, the believers have the same mind because of their connection with Christ Jesus. What they share in common is not a
consensus on a given number of issues; what binds them together
is their being in Christ.

This idea is common across the Pauline corpus: Christians
come together not because of some social club mentality. Rather
Christians share this: God's love was shown to them while they
were all sinners, helpless. Or, as Paul sometimes puts it, they are
brothers because Christ died for them (Rom. 14:15–16 and 1 Cor.
8:11).

In Philippians the hymn of Christ is introduced in 2:6 as a re-
minder to the Philippians that their being of the same mind is
possible not by some collective action of will but because all of
them are in Christ Jesus. Their being in Christ Jesus defines what
it means to be of the same mind and makes the same-mindedness
possible. The Philippians are to look to Christ as the basis for
their being of one mind. Christ, though never a partner with the
Christians in the *societas,* is the basis. The Philippians are one-
minded together because they already find themselves one-
minded together in Christ. Being in Christ is the *sine qua non* of
Paul's *societas.*

Christian community, as far as it can be expressed in the
societas imagery, is firmly grounded in God's action in Christ.
Justified sinners find themselves in right relation to God in Christ.
God's love in Christ makes community possible where there was
formerly merely self-interest governed by the power of sin. In
Christ, Christians are given to one another. In Christ, Christians
are freed to seek the best for others. Paul finds *societas* concepts
such as one-mindedness a viable way of expressing what he and
the Philippian Christians know to be true about themselves in
Christ. In the process, Paul uses the hymn of 2:6 ff. to remind the
Christians that their life in the community has Christ as its foundation. Only *in Christ* is it possible. If all the Philippians abandon

seeking their own self-interests and turn in service to one another, then they will be truly of one mind. The *societas* is indeed *societas Christi*.

Though the occasion in Philippians 2 does not call for it, Paul is capable elsewhere of expanding the notion of *societas* in yet one further direction. Apart from being the foundation of *societas*, Christ is also preached as the goal of *societas*. The preaching of the good news in Christ is the other part of the purpose of *societas*. The Christians can therefore understand *societas* to help them conceptualize two important facets of their common life: (1) the *societas* aids them in understanding how they should live together as partners in Christ and (2) *societas* has a goal that reaches out beyond the borders of their own collective self-interest. We have already seen the second aspect of *societas* in the outcome of the Jerusalem conference and in the Philippians' sending support for Paul's preaching. Paul has been the means of the Philippians' common expression of the gospel. He thereby deserves their support. They give it freely; he accepts it joyfully. Their faith speaks through Paul.

To return briefly to Euodia and Syntyche (4:2), we can now see that Paul's exhortation of them to be of one mind has some specificity that they and their fellow Christians will be able to apply to the particulars of their difficulty. Far from being exhorted to some mystical union,[38] they are called to live with one another as chapter 2 has expressed it in so many ways: in love, in accord, seeking each other's interests, not in self-service or conceit. Paul does not prescribe *what* in particular Euodia and Syntyche are to do. *To auto phronein* does not carry that freight. One could freely paraphrase Paul's exhortation to these two women: "Let your lives be in conformity to the commitment that brought you together in the first place." As long as that commitment continues, their lives together will be governed by it. *To auto phronein* tells them more about *how* they should live together. If they *phronein* together, their common love for one another will find a means of expression.

Further, Euodia and Syntyche are not just any two people in the Philippian congregation; they are fellow workers (*sunergoi*) with Paul and Clement (4:3). They have *sunēthlēsan moi*, "fought at my side," in the gospel. Apparently they too are missionaries of some sort and perhaps, like Paul, they should be understood as having been representatives of the *societas* in the spreading of the gospel.

In his rather typical fashion, Paul aids the reader by an antithetical expression relating to *phronein*. Declaring that he presses on towards the goal (*brabeion*)[39] of the calling (3:14), Paul declares: "Let those of us who are mature be thus minded" (*hosoi oun teleioi, touto phronōmen*). The expression amounts to an invitation for the Philippians to join Paul in this pursuit. It freely mixes *societas* terminology with the image of a prize awarded in the games (note Gal. 2 where we already have seen that combination of running with *societas*). How would one express it if people were not of the same mind? Paul knows and shows it in his next statement: "If in anything you are otherwise minded [*ei ti heterōs phroneite*], God will reveal that also to you" (3:15). The antithesis to being of the same mind may be expressed, as it was in chapter 2, in terms of inappropriate postures such as self-seeking and conceit (2:3 and 2:4), but Paul can settle for the more general expression *heterōs phroneite*, "otherwise minded."[40] Just a few verses later Paul calls Syntyche and Euodia away from this *heterōs phronein* to *to auto phronein*, from being other-minded to being of the same mind.

Of course, Paul takes the matter over into his theological reflection. He tells the Philippians that if they are other-minded in any particular, "God will reveal that also to you" (3:15). Conduct in the *societas Christi* is not simply monitored by the other partners. God will show them when they are other-minded. This same thought is developed in the following verses. There are those, Paul says, who "live as enemies of the cross of Christ" (3:18). Tearfully, Paul describes them: "Their end is destruction, their god is the belly, and they glory in their shame" (3:19). At the root of their difficulty, Paul sees that they *phronein* earthly things: "with minds set on earthly things" (3:19). So it is to be *heterōs phronein*, to be other-minded. Paul then reminds the Philippians that they should "join in imitating" him. If they do so, they will *phronein* not earthly things but "our commonwealth . . . in heaven" (3:20).

Finally on *phronein* in Philippians, when the *societas Christi* functions as it ought to the reciprocity of relationships can even be expressed by Paul through the *phronein* terminology. Here Paul moves beyond its more fundamental *societas* usage of continued agreement about the goal that constituted the *societas* in the first instance. Now Paul pushes the *phronein* words into an expression of the mutuality of the Christian community. Paul can show it towards the Philippians. "It is right for me to feel [*touto phronein*] thus about you all" (1:7). In a similar way, when things are going right the Philippians can express it towards Paul: "I rejoice in the Lord greatly that now at length you have revived your concern for me [*to huper emou phronein*]; you were indeed concerned for me, but you had no opportunity" (4:10, *eph' hō kai ephroneite ēkaireisthe de*, "you were indeed concerned, but you were not presented with the right occasion"). As is clear from the opening verses of chapter 2, Paul has shown that *to auto phronein*, being "of the same mind," is elaborated by "having the same love, being of one accord." The Philippians have shown themselves of the same mind with Paul by sending him the support for his preaching mission. Paul knows it is right for him to *phronein* the Philippians because he holds them in his heart, and even more fundamentally he knows them all to be partakers (*sugkoinōnous*, "joint partners") with him of grace. Paul affirms his proper-mindedness to the Philippians right at the start, between two references to their *koinōnia/societas* relationship to him (1:5, 7).

Paul had an unusually good relationship with the Philippians. He told them so, and the general tone of the letter corroborates that view. The singularity of that relationship can only be appreciated when Philippians is viewed in comparison with the other authentic letters.

The good relationship gained expression when Paul and some of the residents of that ancient Roman colony, Philippi, joined with one another in a consensual *societas*. Actually, we have seen that Paul did enter into *societas* with others, such as the Jerusalem pillars, but only with the Philippians did he have a *societas* that included actual financial support of Paul as their evangelistic messenger to the world that lay beyond their border. From the very start, from the first time they heard the gospel, the Philippians joined Paul in this partnership. We know of three times that they sent Paul support for his preaching as their representative. No other church did that, according to Paul.

In our effort to uncover some particulars of this special relationship, we were greatly aided by the preservation of Paul's receipt for the third of these payments in support of his preaching. Once that is established, other features of the letter come into a new light. The terse admonitions to Euodia and Syntyche to be of the same mind are now understandable. Furthermore, the frequent appearance of *phronein,* the basic word in the phrase "of the same mind," in Philippians is now comprehensible. Not some phrase appealing for or describing mystical experience, being "of the same mind" is language of contract performance that Paul and the Philippians have loaded with special christological significance. Along this line the introduction to the hymn of Christ shows how Paul integrates this *societas* terminology of "being of the same mind" with his more widely known categories. To be "of the same mind" is like having "the same love" or like being "in full accord and of one mind" (*sumpsychoi*) (2:2). It means rejecting selfishness, conceit, and self-serving, a rejection made possible by Christ's action for the believers (Phil. 2:6–11). It entails humility and caring about the matters that relate to others. These more typically Pauline phrases stand right alongside the less frequent "be of the same mind" and help us understand how the

71

latter functioned to express the way the Philippian Christians were to live with one another in true and full partnership in Christ.

The Philippians and Paul understood themselves as *societas Christi*. With them he entered into a partnership (*societas*) that involved both living with one another as brothers and sisters and spreading the gospel. Paul becomes the chief means by which the Philippians carry out the latter goal of the partnership. The extant letter to them thanks them for their repeated efforts in support of him and encourages them to continue to live out the terms of the partnership in their daily lives together.

Paul declares that only with the Philippians did he have a *societas* that entailed giving and receiving. Accordingly, only there can we expect to see his bookkeeping. We can, however, expect to see the *societas* model, or at least parts of it, invoked in other Pauline correspondence.

NOTES

1. Two classic studies of colonial Philippi should be noted: Paul Collart, *Philippes Ville de Macédoine* (Paris: E. de Boccard, 1937), and Paul Lemerle, *Philippes et la Macédoine Orientale* (Paris: E. de Boccard, 1945).

2. Collart, *Philippes Ville de Macédoine*, pp. 300–301: "Certes, dès le Ier siècle avant notre ère, le latin s'était imposé sur tout le territoire de la colonie. C'était non seulement la langue officielle, qui s'affichait, sur le forum, au front des édifices, sur les monuments dédiés aux dieux, sur les bases gravées pour honorer d'illustres personnages, et dans laquelle s'énonçaient les titres des magistratures municipales." He holds that the same is true for the back country.

3. Lemerle, *Philippes et la Macédoine Orientale*, p. 302.

4. For an accounting of the Roman and Greek mixture of the populace, see ibid., p. 13.

5. Jean Fleury, "Une Société de Fait dans l'Église Apostolique (Phil. 4:10 à 22)," in *Mélanges Philippe Meylan*, vol. 2, *Histoire du Droit* (Lausanne: Lausanne Université, 1963), p. 49: "Il faut d'ailleurs préciser qu'il n'est pas nécessaire que les associés aient eu tous la qualité de citoyens romains pour qu'ils aient eu recours à une société

de type romain entre eux. Ils pouvaient le faire à l'imitation de ce qui se faisait habituellement autour d'eux."

6. Debates concerning the literary integrity of Philippians continue but do not directly affect our argument. For literature on this discussion, however, see W. G. Kümmel, *Introduction to the New Testament,* 17th ed. (Nashville: Abingdon Press, 1973), pp. 332–35.

7. See above, p. 15.

8. F. W. Beare, *A Commentary on the Epistle to the Philippians* (New York: Harper & Row, 1959), pp. 149–57.

9. *TDNT,* s.v. *"apechō":* "to have received what is owed," "normally used for receipts." Cf. Adolf Deissmann, *Light from the Ancient East,* 4th ed. (New York: George H. Doran Co., 1927), p. 111: "I think we may say, therefore, that this technical meaning of *apechō* . . . must have been known to every Greek-speaking person, down to the meanest labourer." So also J. H. Moulton and G. Milligan, *The Vocabulary of the Greek New Testament,* 2d ed. (London: Hodder and Stoughton, 1915), p. 57.

10. Beare, *Philippians,* p. 150.

11. Fleury, "Une Société de Fait," p. 53.

12. F. Wilbur Gingrich and Frederick W. Danker, eds., *A Greek-English Lexicon of the New Testament,* 2d ed. rev. (Grand Rapids: Zondervan Publishing House, 1979), p. 478.

13. Henry G. Liddell and Robert Scott, eds., *Greek-English Lexicon,* 9th ed. (Oxford: Oxford University Press, 1940), p. 444.

14. Ibid., p. 2002. See Fleury, "Une Société de Fait," pp. 53–54, on *chreia* in *societas* context.

15. For corpus harmonization at its worst concerning Phil. 4:14–19, cf. C. H. Dodd, "The Mind of Paul:I," in *New Testament Studies* (New York: Charles Scribner's Sons, n.d.), pp. 71–72: "Here Paul is trying to say a graceful word of thanks for a gift of money. How much he hated taking it, we may infer from 1 Cor. 9.15–18. He can scarcely bring himself to acknowledge that the money was welcome to him, and covers up his embarrassment by piling up technical terms of trade, as if to give the transaction a severely 'business' aspect." J. B. Lightfoot, *St. Paul's Epistle to the Philippians,* 2d ed. (London: Macmillan & Co., 1869), pp. 165–66, also brings Philippians into line with the rest of the corpus: "The limitation *en archē tou euaggeliou* [4:15] perhaps implies that he relaxed his rule later, when he became better known and understood."

16. W. W. Buckland, *A Text-book of Roman Law from Augustus to Justinian* (Cambridge: Cambridge University Press, 1921), pp. 506:

"They [partners, *socii*] were bound to account for receipts on firm business and entitled to contribution for expenses properly incurred."

17. See H. A. Fischel, "Stoicism," in *Encyclopaedia Judaica* (New York: Macmillan, 1971), 15: 409–10 and his bibliography; cf. also his "Cynics and Cynicism," ibid., 5: 1177–78. See also John M. Rist, *Stoic Philosophy* (London: Cambridge University Press, 1969).

18. J. N. Sevenster, *Paul and Seneca* (Leiden: E. J. Brill, 1961), esp. pp. 113–14.

19. F. Hauck, *"karpos," TDNT* 3:614–16: "consequence, result, profit" (p. 615). Cf. Beare, *Philippians*, p. 155.

20. Lightfoot, *Epistle to the Philippians*, p. 165: "*doseōs kai lēmpseōs*, 'giving and taking,' 'credit and debit,' a general expression for pecuniary transactions, derived from the two sides of the ledger. . . . The phrase refers solely to the passing of money between the two."

21. On the bookkeeping terminology, cf. also Fleury, "Une Société de Fait," pp. 51–52.

22. G. Kittel, *"logos," TDNT* 4:104: "It is particularly plain in Phil. 4:15, 17 to what degree the term has in this sense the tendency to move out of the commercial sphere as a figure of spiritual things. The *logos* ('account') *doseōs kai lēmpseōs* (v. 15) which first applies to earthly things, i.e., support of the apostle, unexpectedly becomes an image of the *karpon ton pleonazonta eis logon humōn* (v. 17), i.e., fruit in a very different eternal sense since the earthly goods are reckoned as equivalent to the spiritual gift received."

23. Lightfoot, *Epistle to the Philippians*, p. 167. Concerning *osmēn euōdias* he writes: "A very frequent expression in the LXX for the smell of sacrifices and offerings, being a rendering of *rêᵃh nîhoāh* (e.g., Gen. 8:21, Exod. 29:18, etc.). St. Paul employs it as a metaphor likewise in Ephes. 5:2; cf. 2 Cor. 2:15, 16."

24. Fleury, "Une Société de Fait," pp. 41–59. Only after I "discovered" *societas* in Philippians did I find that Fleury had played Native Americans to my Columbus.

25. Fleury is absolutely sound concerning the capacity of any partner to terminate *societas*. As we shall see, Fleury's reading of Phil. 4:17 is neither the only one nor the most likely one.

26. Deissmann, *Light from the Ancient East*, p. 112, n. 1: "*Apechō* is frequently combined with *panta* in receipts."

27. Hans Conzelmann, *1 Corinthians*, trans. James W. Leitch (Philadelphia: Fortress Press, 1975), p. 154, n. 29, in commenting on Paul's refusal to accept support from the Corinthians (9:1 ff.), notes that 2 Cor. 11:7 ff. and Phil. 4:10 ff. "show that Paul accepts maintenance in

other cases. He does not make a principle of his renunciation, but behaves on each occasion as the case requires." Cf. *TDNT*, s.v. *"perisseuō."*

28. Moulton and Milligan, *Vocabulary*, p. 351, recognize a wide range of usage for *koinōnia* and *koinōnos*. Among those, they note that both are used as contract and partnership terms.

29. Lightfoot, *Epistle to the Philippians*, p. 83, concerning *epi tē koinōnia*: "The words signify not 'your participation in the gospel' . . . but 'your cooperation [I would translate "partnership"] towards, in aid of the Gospel.'"

30. C. J. Ellicott, *A Critical and Grammatical Commentary on St. Paul's Epistles to the Philippians, Colossians, and to Philemon* (Boston: Draper and Halliday, 1866), p. 21, translates 1:5 as "partnership in reference to the gospel," "the *eis* marking the object toward which the *koinōnia* was directed."

31. With the exception of the situation reflected in Phil. 3:2 ff., where Paul strikes out in harsh strokes against some threat to Philippian unity. It is precisely in these verses that many find some of the strongest evidence against the unity of canonical Philippians. Cf. Kümmel, *Introduction*, pp. 332–35.

32. Gingrich, and Danker, eds., *Greek-English Lexicon*, p. 866. Cf. *TDNT*, s.v. *"phroneō, phronēma."* Cf. also Adolf Deissmann, *Bible Studies* (Edinburgh: T. & T. Clark, 1909), p. 256, concerning *to auto phronein*: "This formula and others of similar formation which are current in the writings of the Apostle Paul have been found in Herodotus and other writers. The epitaph IMAe. 149 (Rhodes, 2d cent. B.C.), in which it is said of a married couple *tauta legontes tauta phronountes ēlthomen tan ametrēton hodon eis Aidan*, permits of the supposition that it was familiarly used in popular speech."

33. The most comprehensive survey of general trends in modern interpretation of the hymn is that of R. P. Martin, *Carmen Christi: Philippians 2:5–11 in Recent Interpretation and in the Setting of Early Christian Worship* (Cambridge: Cambridge University Press, 1967). See esp. chap. 4, "Main Lines of Twentieth-Century Interpretation," pp. 63–95. To oversimplify, there are two dominant interpretations. The one reads the hymn with Christ as example and is referred to as the ethical or moral reading; the second reads it "in terms of soteriology, not Christology . . . what Christ did, not what he was" (p. 83). Käsemann has led the assault against reading the hymn as presenting Christ as a pattern to be emulated. Martin finally follows Käsemann. The interpreter ought to "dismiss the idea that Christ is set forth as an

example. . . . Verse 5 therefore introduces a hymn with the apostolic preface that the Philippians are to act one to another as is fitting to those who are in the sphere of Christ's rule as his people." So Martin, p. 85. I think Käsemann and Martin are fundamentally right. Christ is after all not the pattern for the *societas*; he is its very foundation, its basis. Cf. G. Strecker, "Redaktion und Tradition im Christus-Hymnus Phil 2," *ZNW* 55 (1964): 63–78, who argues that the either-or debate concerning ethical or christological interpretation of the hymn is overdone and based on wrong alternatives. Both matters are present, he maintains. Cf. also O. Hofius, *Der Christushymnus Phil 2,6–11*, Untersuchungen zur Gestalt und Aussage eines urchristlichen Psalms (Tübingen: J. C. B. Mohr [Paul Siebeck], 1976).

34. Ellicott, *A Critical and Grammatical Commentary*, p. 51: "The following participial clauses [after *to auto phronēte* in 2:2] . . . more nearly define its essence and characteristics."

35. Lightfoot, *Epistle to the Philippians*, p. 108, calls *dexias edōkan* "a general expression of accordance, which is defined and enforced by the three following clauses. It is the concord not of a common hatred, but of a common love. It manifests itself in a complete harmony of the feelings and affections. It produces an entire unison of thought and directs to one end. The redundancy of expression is a measure of the Apostle's earnestness."

36. Ibid. *To hen phronounte*, concluding 2:2, is "a stronger expression than the foregoing *to auto phronēte*, from which it does not otherwise differ."

37. Phil. 2:5 has caused interpreters difficulty. C. F. D. Moule, "Further Reflections on Philippians 2:5–11," in *Apostolic History and the Gospel: Biblical and Historical Essays presented to F. F. Bruce*, ed. W. W. Gasque and R. P. Martin (Grand Rapids: Eerdmans, 1970), p. 265, reports that many translate 2:5 "something like 'adopt towards one another, in your mutual relations, the same attitude as you adopt towards Christ Jesus, in your union with him.'" Moule offers instead: "Adopt towards one another, in your mutual relations, the same attitude which was found in Christ Jesus." Martin, *Carmen Christi*, p. 289: "It is permissible to read the cryptic words [of 2:5b] as implying that Paul is summoning the Philippians to act in such a way as befits their standing in Christ Jesus, i.e., as members of his Church [I would say 'as partners']." Martin, p. 289, n. 1, continues: "In other words, this attitude of mind (described in verses 1–4) they are to have in their personal relations because it is the only attitude proper to those who are 'in Christ.'" Martin is sound enough here

but has settled too much for an attitudinal interpretation of *to auto phronein* and Phil. 2:1–4. A *way of life together* is described in 2:1–4. Anything less empties the passage and the *phronein* terminology of *societas*.

30. Lucien Cerfaux, *Le Chrétien dans la Théologie Paulinienne* (Paris: Editions du Cerf, 1962), p. 303, n. 1, declares that Paul's use of *koinōnia* sometimes tempts him to translate it as "union mystique." Our study of *societas* suggests that such a translation in Philippians would be absolutely erroneous.

39. Victor C. Pfitzner, *Paul and the Agon Motif* (Leiden: E. J. Brill, 1967), pp. 139–56.

40. *P.Oxy.* 282 and *P.Bon.* 21 reflect similar situations. The wife of each author has become alienated from her husband. This alienation is expressed by *allotria phronēsasa* (*P.Oxy.* 282.9) and by *allotria phronēsas* (*P.Bon.* 21.8). I quote *P.Oxy.* 282.6–10: "I for my part provided for my wife in a manner that exceeded my resources. But she became dissatisfied with [of another mind concerning] our union."

5

Further Reflections of *Societas* in the Pauline Correspondence

When searching across the remaining Pauline corpus to see whether Paul actually established *societas* with any other Christians, the possibilities narrow rather quickly. Considered one at a time, most of the remaining Pauline letters either show no definite signs of *societas Christi* or manifest conditions of hostility and mistrust that are fundamentally alien to the establishment or continuance of *societas*.

With the Letter to Philemon, however, we find the terminology of *societas* in a third Pauline letter. The key verse in this document is 17 (NEB): "If, then, you count me your partner in the faith [*ei oun me echeis koinōnon*], welcome him as you would welcome me." The letter is so brief and the evidence is so limited that we cannot with any degree of certainty conclude whether Paul actually had a formal *societas* with Philemon. If he did not, at least Paul uses the *societas* partnership language as a way of focusing the central issue for Philemon. In accord with *societas*, Paul describes how he is going to relate to Philemon and suggests that Philemon must decide how he will respond to Onesimus. It is striking that the pivotal verse in the letter (v. 17) resorts to the *societas* pattern and declares (literally): "If, therefore, you consider me partner (*koinōnon*), receive him as me."

The runaway slave Onesimus has been converted by Paul's preaching while the latter was in prison. Now the slave is sent

back to his master, Philemon, with a letter from Paul.[1] In a sense
it is a letter of introduction—even though the two men, slave and
master, know each other from before—because Onesimus now
comes to Philemon as a new person, as Paul's child in Christ.[2] So
the letter is sent to one person—in a Christian church[3]—converted
by Paul, namely, Philemon, who owes Paul "even your own self"
(v. 19), concerning another Pauline convert, Onesimus. Significantly, the grace with which the letter opens (v. 3) recognizes
that God is the Father of the faithful. In accord with this, Paul
can address Philemon as "brother" in verse 20. It is also in this
sense that Paul reintroduces Onesimus no longer simply as Philemon's slave but now "more than a slave, as a beloved brother,
especially to me but how much more to you" (v. 16). People of
very different social strata are now brothers in Christ, a radical
application of the kinship character of the gospel (cf. Gal. 3:7)
and thoroughly in accord with *societas*.[4] Philemon is to receive
Onesimus "as me" (*hōs eme*), as a brother in Christ.[5] Philemon
will do that if he retains partnership (*societas*) with Paul (v. 17).
The partners are also the brothers.

Paul's authority and boldness in Christ would allow him "to
command you to do what is required" (v. 8)[6] but Paul explicitly
rejects that approach (cf. also v. 14)[7] In place of command, Paul
prefers exhortation, appeal.[8] A good deed (*to agathon sou*, "good-
ness," RSV, v. 14) might be achieved by Paul's command and
Philemon's consent, but true partners do not command. For
societas partners there is reciprocity and mutual good faith. Pre-
serving that reciprocity and Philemon's freedom, Paul renounces
the mode of command so that Philemon's good deed "might not
be by compulsion but of your own free will" (v. 14).

What Philemon's good deed might be is not prescribed. Philemon must determine that. In this instance the shape of love is
not defined by Paul. If Philemon would retain his partnership
with Paul (v. 17),[9] then Philemon will show that same love and
faith for which he is famous "toward the Lord Jesus and all the
saints" (v. 5) toward one of God's newer saints, Onesimus. What

should Philemon do to Onesimus? If Philemon has *societas* with Paul, then Philemon should "receive him as me" (v. 17).

In an effort to remove any hindrance to Philemon's welcoming his new brother, Paul promises Philemon to cover any wrong or loss that Philemon may have suffered when Onesimus left him earlier (vv. 18-19). This little additional contract is not to be confused with *societas*. As was the case in the appearance of *societas* in Philippians, so also in Philemon the legal language of bookkeeping and accounting may be found alongside and inter-twined with the terminology of *societas*. The promissory note of verses 18-19 should remove any pecuniary concern from Phile-mon so that he may be even freer to let love do its work in the return of Onesimus. The matter is in Philemon's hands. All hin-drances are removed so that Philemon may confront the central issue: does he wish to retain his partnership with Paul? If he has *societas* with Paul, Philemon will accept his runaway slave Onesimus as a beloved brother, as he would receive Paul himself.

WIDER POSSIBLE MARKS OF *SOCIETAS* ON THE PAULINE CORRESPONDENCE

Even in those letters where *societas* is impossible or improbable because the conditions basic to it are absent, we can see that Paul employs *societas* terminology—though his readers do not neces-sarily understand themselves in partnership with Paul. In particu-lar there are three matters where *societas* may have made a wider mark across the Pauline correspondence: (1) Paul's personal and public finances, (2) Paul's absence and properly qualified repre-sentatives sent in his stead, and (3) Paul's establishment of the norm of satisfactory conduct in the performance of obligations.

Paul's Personal and Public Finances

Paul's personal and public finances were a matter of friction and misconception. All of these misunderstandings are either caused by or connected with *societas*. The questions about Paul's finances center around two matters: the collection for the Jeru-

81

salem sainted poor and Paul's acceptance or nonacceptance of support for his preaching the gospel.

The collection for the poor is mentioned in four of Paul's letters, Romans, 1 and 2 Corinthians, and Galatians, and is of course the one requirement the Jerusalem pillars put on Paul and Barnabas as they all entered into a *societas* for the preaching of the gospel (Gal. 2:10). Several problems seem to have arisen in connection with the collection. From the clues in the letters, let us reconstruct Paul's efforts concerning the collection. In writing to the Corinthians, Paul reports that he "ordered" (*dietaxa*, 1 Cor. 16:1) the churches of Galatia to begin setting aside something for the collection on the first day of every week. And he writes the Corinthians: "So you also are to do" (1 Cor. 16:1 ff.). In a later correspondence with the Corinthians, Paul describes to them how the Macedonians, though poor and troubled, responded with zeal concerning the collection: "begging us earnestly for the favor of taking part" (2 Cor. 8:4). Thus we see that the collection was instituted by Paul's directive in two Roman provinces, Galatia and Achaia, and reportedly engaged in voluntarily by Christians in a third Roman province, Macedonia.

Problems arose. The Corinthians, who readily began to take part (2 Cor. 8:10) and who promised to make a gift for the collection (2 Cor. 9:5), lost their enthusiasm for it. Paul, in his subsequent correspondence with them about the collection, withdraws from the directive posture reflected in 1 Corinthians 16:1 and in fact openly eschews command: "I say this not as a command" (2 Cor. 8:8); "And in this matter I give my advice" (2 Cor. 8:10); and "Each one must do as he has made up his mind, not reluctantly or under compulsion" (2 Cor. 9:7).

Paul had taken precautions to avoid suspicion concerning his handling of the collection. When he first wrote of it to the Corinthians, he indicated his expectation that they would want to send certified representatives along with their gift to Jerusalem (surely not an extraordinary practice in those times).[10] At some point in the two- or three-year process of gathering this collection, "the churches"—which ones are not known—appointed (*cheirotonē-theis*) a "famous [*epainos*] brother" who had earned his mark "among all the churches for his preaching of the gospel" (2 Cor. 8:18) to travel along with Paul as he went about soliciting and gathering the collection. Though Paul does not give the name of this person, it is safe to assume that the Corinthians knew who he was, and one may conjecture that they might have had a hand in his "appointment." At any rate, the selection of this well-respected outsider to the Pauline camp suggests a concern on the part of the churches for an overseer of the Pauline collection. Paul has obviously consented to it—"to show our good will" (2 Cor. 8:19)—and mentions the man precisely because Paul is now sending him back with Titus to be on hand (and perhaps lend support) as Titus shapes matters up in Corinth regarding the collection. Paul takes every possible step to assuage the Corinthian fears and misgivings about this operation for which they had such initial zeal and encourages them in this test (2 Cor. 9:13).[12]

Not only was the collection itself marked by much misunderstanding and misgivings on the part of Paul's churches; it was a limited success. Macedonia and Achaia did finally take part, Macedonia with no apparent reticence. But it is evident from Paul's Letter to the Romans that the Galatians never did join in the collection despite Paul's command of them to do so (1 Cor. 16:1). In Romans Paul writes that he has concluded his evangelistic work in the regions near the eastern Mediterranean and is prepared to move via Rome to the west. He has the collection in hand, reports that he is personally taking it to Jerusalem, and indicates that it came from the generosity of the Macedonian and Achaian churches (Rom. 15:26).[13]

Thus Paul carries out his obligation under the Jerusalem *societas* to remember the poor but does so with somewhat limited success and not without causing some misunderstanding as he went, particularly among the Corinthians. But the collection is not the only financial matter that raised Corinthian suspicion regarding Paul. Paul's personal finances presented problems as well.

Paul did not have a set policy concerning the financing of his preaching mission. From some he accepted support for his preaching; from others he pointedly refused it. In some places he appears to have adopted a pattern of maintaining himself by his trade while preaching the gospel as opportunity presented itself (1 Thess. 2:9); in other places there is no clue that he plied his trade. Problems arose when different churches found out that Paul was not consistent in this matter. Who can wonder that the Corinthians were a bit nonplussed when Paul, who adamantly and consistently refused to accept any support from *them* even though he was in need (2 Cor. 11:9), readily accepted the assistance "supplied by the brethren who came from Macedonia" (2 Cor. 11:9)?

Two predictable but divergent responses apparently arose in Corinth as a result of the Macedonian aid. From the one side Paul is accused of "robbing other churches" (2 Cor. 11:8). From the other side there is some grumbling by the Corinthians that they are not allowed to support Paul (2 Cor. 11:10 and 2 Cor. 12:13). We know from the Letter to the Philippians that they have had a continuing policy of sending support to Paul as their representative in the *societas Christi* (Phil. 4:10–20). Those gift-payments occasion the two-pronged misunderstanding of the Corinthians.

The diversity of Paul's financial relationships with his different Christian communities has been glossed over by an homogenous— corpus harmonization again—picture of Paul as tentmaker regularly plying his trade in his preaching the gospel.[14] Two factors have contributed to that unsupported though popular, uniform picture. Of prime importance no doubt is the portrait of Paul in Acts, particularly in the description of his time with Priscilla and Aquila (Acts 18:1–3): "And he went to see them [in Corinth]; and because he was of the same trade he stayed with them, and they worked, for by trade they were tentmakers." Other passages in Acts tend to confirm the impression that Paul's regular pattern was to support himself by his trade while carrying on his preaching: "You yourselves know that these hands ministered to my necessities, and to those who were with me" (Acts 20:34).

Paul's letters are usually read as confirming the Acts pattern. In fact, however, only two of the unquestioned Pauline letters explicitly refer to his working at a trade while preaching the gospel.[15] To the Corinthians, who are exulting in their new status and freedom in Christ, Paul shows by ironic contrast that he has not been admitted to their pretended lofty status. In the context of that passage he declares: "To the present hour we hunger and thirst, we are ill-clad and buffeted and homeless, and we labor, working with our own hands" (1 Cor. 4:11–12a). To the Thessalonians, in less biting tones, he remarks: "For you remember our labor and toil, brethren; we worked night and day, that we might not burden any of you, while we preached to you the gospel of God" (1 Thess. 2:9).

As in all historical circumstances, matters were probably more varied and complex. Clearly, on issues of personal support Paul related differently with different churches. Paul's preaching was supported by at least two means: Paul worked at a trade from time to time, and he accepted aid from the Macedonians on occasion. We have no basis to assume that Paul "set up shop" in each city where he established a church. Previously earned goods or outside support could have carried him at several junctures.

Even though Paul avers that he would never accept any support from the Corinthians, he is careful to claim that it is still his right even though he refuses to exercise it. Already in 1 Corinthians there is some question of Paul's right to support. As Paul understands it the question impinges on his role as apostle. That he labels his response a "defense" is clear evidence that he is under attack (1 Cor. 9:3). Paul introduces the question of his own right (*exousia*) to support as an object lesson for the Corinthians. As he is free *not* to use his right, so the "strong" Corinthians should exercise *their* freedom by not harming the "weak," that is, by giving up their *exousia* to eat meat when it might cause the weak to stumble. His response, though rather lengthily developed, may be summarized: Apostles are due support for their work. Experience shows that this is true in other enterprises, such as soldiering, vintnering, and shepherding. Torah also supports it. So does temple practice. And finally, the Corinthians themselves, by their treatment of other apostles "and the brothers of the Lord and Cephas" (1 Cor. 9:5), show they know support to be an apostolic right. Paul concludes this phase of his argument by asking rhetorically: "If others share this rightful claim upon you, do not we still more?" (1 Cor. 9:12). So it is Paul's right (*exousia*) to receive support for his preaching of the gospel to the Corinthians, but Paul steadfastly refuses to exercise the right with them.[16] His insistence on his right, however, must not be taken as an oblique request to them (1 Cor. 9:15). Even with that disclaimer, the notion still haunts some Corinthians that Paul is not really interested in them as much as he is in their support This he has to deny also: "Here for the third time I am ready to come to you. And I will not be a burden, for I seek not what is yours but you" (2 Cor. 12:14).

Caught in the crossfire of the Corinthian attacks and doubts, Paul continues to affirm not only his apostolic right of support but also his freedom to refrain from exercising that rightful claim. Significantly, at no point in the Corinthian correspondence does Paul adduce *societas* categories in support of his right as an apostle. Instead he refers to the common practices of the day in the army, vineyards, and oversight of cattle. He quotes Torah, refers to temple practice, and even quotes Jesus in support of his right.

Societas would have supported that right as well. Why did Paul not use that point also since he is piling up arguments for his case? We have established that the conditions requisite to *societas* were absent with the Corinthian Christians. In contrast, Paul can accept support over and over from the Philippians, with whom he has been in partnership from the very beginning.[17] They are partners, and he is due their support for work done in behalf of the partnership. Never is there any clue that the Philippians have been confused about that. But with the Corinthians Paul lacked the untarnished good faith and simple trust that he enjoyed with the Philippians. Among Corinthians the *societas* argument would have been out of place. Paul has to resort to other arguments with them. But the Corinthian questions about Paul's personal finances serve as a barometer of his relationship to them and, by contrast, highlight the fuller, more secure relationship that he enjoyed with the Philippians. It is no wonder that some Corinthians began to grumble that Paul favored some of his other churches.

Paul's Absence and Properly Qualified Representatives in His Stead

In a world where communication was poor and sometimes haphazard, what happened to contracts when one or more of the parties was incommunicado for a time? Was there a statute of limitations beyond which the partners were relieved of their responsibilities and the partnership dissolved? The matter is pressing in the study of Paul when one notes the many projected but frustrated, unrealized visits.[18] To set the issue more concretely in terms of our study, could Paul's protracted absence from Philippi put an end to his *societas* with them? Is there such a provision in Roman legal traditions? To my knowledge there is not.[19] Absence alone does not necessarily terminate *societas*.

Although absence apparently does not terminate the contract, one's absence can be alleviated by the function of carefully chosen emissaries. In a legal tradition credited to Sabinus, a Roman jurist contemporary with Paul, Ulpian declares:

> A similar consideration applies where the reason why one of the partners threw up the connexion was that he would have to be absent on state business for a long time and against his will. It is true that there might be cases in which he would lay himself open to the remark that he was able to carry on the partnership business equally well by an agent, or entrust the management to his co-partner; still this would only be admissible where the co-partner was a man of exceptional ability, or the party who meant

to absent himself could easily carry on the business even by the hands of an agent (*Digest* 17. 2. 16).[20]

The situation in view in this legal text is one of a partner (*socius*) who determines to end his partnership—a step fully within the rights of any partner. His reason is that he will be absent for some time, against his will.

The partner who of his own volition absents himself can easily carry on the partnership through another member of the partnership (*per alium societatis administratio*). For the partner who is absent without willing it, say on state business or under force, there are two possibilities: first, he cannot be held legally responsible for the partnership, and the obligations of the partnership may go unmet; or, second, he may carry on the partnership through representatives, though only if these men are "of exceptional ability." In either case—whether the absence is voluntary or not—a partner may carry on the business of the partnership through the efforts of others.

Paul's letters ring out a litany of protracted absences due to plans that do not come to fruition. His absences are not of his own willing. Predominantly in the Pauline correspondence it is "the Lord" who determines where and when Paul travels and who accordingly is responsible for Paul's absence. Paul wishes to see various churches, but the Lord whom he serves does not allow him to visit them at the moment. For example, Paul writes the Corinthians that he "hopes to spend some time" with them, "if the Lord permits" (1 Cor. 16:7). The identical theme is sounded earlier in the same letter: "I will come to you soon, if the Lord wills" (4:19). A similar motif appears in Philemon where "the Lord" is not specifically mentioned but may surely be understood: "At the same time, prepare a guest room for me, for I am hoping through your prayers to be granted to you" (Phlem. 22).

Paul is not the free master of his fate. As he so often declares, he is a slave to Christ. He does not his own will but the bidding of his master. His absence from his fellow Christians, therefore, is not an absence that can simply be construed as voluntary. Some

Christians seem to have taken it as such and accuse Paul of vacillation in his intention to visit them. But he denies it: "I wanted to visit you on my way to Macedonia, and to come back to you from Macedonia and have you send me on my way to Judea. Was I vacillating when I wanted to do this? Do I make my plans like a worldly man, ready to say Yes and No at once? As surely as God is faithful, our word to you has not been Yes and No" (2 Cor. 1:15–18).[21] It is as if Paul is making his travel plans as one engaged in state business and under the rule of someone else.

In the opening of Romans Paul declares that he has "often intended to come to you but thus far have been prevented" (1:13). It is reasonable to suppose that it is "the Lord" who has prevented him from doing so. But one cannot be absolutely certain because Paul does ascribe one frustrated visit to the work of Satan. "We wanted to come to you—I, Paul, again and again—but Satan hindered us" (1 Thess. 2:18).

At any rate, Paul's absence from his fellow Christians seems consistently to be against his own will. Most often Paul's absence is the Lord's doing; once it is credited to Satan. As a servant of Christ Paul is caught up beyond the everyday matters of willing and choosing, though his heart would have him present with the recipients of his letters.

These frustrated or delayed visits often eventuate in Paul's sending a representative. *Digest* 17. 2.16, quoted just above, says that the absent partner can send an emissary as long as the person is of exceptional character. Accordingly, desiring to maintain the relationship even though absent against his will, Paul is careful to testify regarding the outstanding merits of the representatives.

We may begin to examine this feature of the Pauline correspondence with Philippians because we know that *societas Christi* was operative between Paul and the Philippians. In Paul's absence on this occasion, Timothy is the representative: "I hope in the Lord Jesus to send Timothy to you soon, so that I may be cheered by news of you. I have no one like him, who will be genuinely anxious for your welfare. They all look after their own interests, not those of Jesus Christ. But Timothy's worth you know, how as a son with a father he has served with me in the gospel. I hope therefore to send him just as soon as I see how it will go with me" (2:19–23). Timothy is commended as exceptional. Others focus on their own concerns; Timothy's special characteristic is his genuine concern for the welfare of the Philippian Christians. They already know him and his worth (dokimē) because, like a son with a father, Timothy has served Paul in the gospel.²²

This commendation of Timothy correlates directly to the societas construction already noted in the opening verses of Philippians 2 (1–5): "They all look after their own interests, not those of Jesus Christ" (2:21).²³ Compare the earlier elaboration of how Christians live together in partnership in Christ: "Do nothing from selfishness or conceit, but in humility count others better than yourselves. Let each of you look not only to his own interests, but also to the interests of others" (2:3–4). One of Timothy's hallmarks is his genuine interest in the Philippians; whereas others look first to their self-interests and not to those of Jesus Christ, Timothy is the opposite.²⁴ He embodies the life of societas Christi—as does Paul himself. So in sending Timothy to the Philippians, Paul very nearly sends his double, like a son in place of a father.²⁵

Thus we see that Paul's Letter to the Philippians, in its commendation of Timothy, is in line with Roman legal provisions concerning a representative in lieu of the absent partner. Such a person may go in one's behalf. In the wider Pauline corpus these rigorous standards for representatives are applied to Titus as well. Titus served as a reporter from the Corinthians to Paul (2 Cor. 7:6) and worked among them as Paul's right-hand man. Paul even refers to Titus as his "partner" (koinōnos/socius, 2 Cor. 8:23) and says of him that God put "the same earnest care for you into the heart of Titus" (2 Cor. 8:16). Titus is Paul's partner and is guided by God or Christ in the same way Paul is.

Timothy and Titus are not only certified positively (they do
the same as Paul); they are also approved by negation (they
avoid the same things that Paul avoids). In one of his many difficult moments with the Corinthians, Paul tries to clear up some
matters by asserting how he and his representatives related to
the Corinthians. Paul did not take advantage of the Corinthians,
he asserts; neither did his representatives: "Did I take advantage
of you through any of those whom I sent to you? I urged Titus to
go, and sent the brother with him. Did Titus take advantage of
you? Did we not act in the same spirit? Did we not take the same
steps?" (2 Cor. 12:17–18).

Paul has been able to turn over the work in the partnership to
those trusted representatives because they too serve the same
master. They walk in the same spirit. They seek the same ends,
as good partners should. They are men of tried and true character. They are, in effect, Paul's doubles.

Even so, Paul does not content himself with representatives.
He still longs to be granted a visit to the recipients of the various
letters and often calls for their prayers with him to that end. In
the meantime, however, while his service to his Lord takes him
in other directions, communications and other matters of the partnership may be carried on through representatives of high character such as Titus and Timothy. By this means Paul can avoid
even the slightest hint that his unwilling absence frees him from
any of his obligations.

Though the Corinthians, the Thessalonians, and the Romans
need not have the full *societas* context to understand the creden-
tials of the representatives, the Philippians can understand it.
And once we see it at work with them, we can see the context out
of which Paul may be working as he relates to the other churches.

The Standard of Conduct in the
Performance of Obligations

The third way in which *societas* may have made a wider mark
on the Pauline correspondence, even though his readers may not

have understood themselves in such a partnership with him, may be seen in the establishment of the norm for satisfactory contract performance. Under Roman law *societas* and three other contracts are considered *bona fides*.[26] A contract is *bona fides* when it is based on good faith, honesty, and straightforwardness between or among the parties. Fraud, deceit, and craftiness would be the counterpart, and the presence of any one of these would obviate any of the four *bonae fidei* contracts of Roman law. In contract law, *fides* depicts not only the performance that one is to make but also suggests what one may reasonably expect from the other party or parties to the contract.[27] *Fides* not only "denotes honest keeping of one's promises and performing the duties assumed by agreement"; it also "means the confidence, trust, faith one has in another's behavior, particularly with regard to the fulfillment of his liabilities."[28]

Across the years of Roman legal history there was some predictable uncertainty concerning the norms for satisfactory conduct in *bonae fidei* contracts. Of course, a given contract might call for particular contributions or actions from the different members, but what was the standard of care required by the different parties to the contract as they performed these duties? What conduct was inappropriate to the "good faith" on which the contract was supposed to be founded? How was the standard of care to be determined? It is difficult to answer these questions because the norm seems to have been in flux as the years went by.

In the period of classical law (150 B.C.E.—235 C.E.), *bona fides* required the *socius* (partner) to perform on the level of the "ordinary man" as the standard. In the postclassical period the individual was expected to manifest "only the care he showed in his own affairs."[29]

On three levels one can see possible reflections of this concern with good faith in Paul's writings. First, he often insists that he did not take advantage of or deceive anyone (1 Thess. 2:3–5; 2 Cor. 12:17–18; 2 Cor. 7:2; 2 Cor. 4:1 ff.); he has kept good faith in the relationship (1 Thess. 2:10 and cf. Gal. 2:21). Second, he

92

reminds his readers of obligations that they undertook in good
faith, that they "began not only to do but to desire" and calls for
their faithful completion of them (2 Cor. 8:10–11). Third, he
certifies that the standards of his relationship to them are not
those of the "ordinary man" (2 Cor. 1:12; 10:2; cf. 1 Cor. 3:3 and
Gal. 1:10); rather the care he shows in his own affairs sets the
pattern his readers are to follow.

In Roman law fraud terminates the *bona fide* contract of consensual *societas*. The technical term for fraud is *dolus*,[30] a Latin
word derived directly from the Greek *dolos*. Apart from the appearance of the term in the vice list of Romans 1, *dolos* appears
twice in the Pauline corpus. Both of the times relate directly to
Paul's behavior towards his churches. One is in the very conten-
tious section of 2 Corinthians (10–13) where legal terms abound
(e.g., "Any charge must be sustained by the evidence of two or
three witnesses," 13:1) and where Paul freely reflects the charges
levelled against him by the Corinthians. Paul writes: "But grant-
ing that I myself did not burden you, I was crafty, you say, and
got the better of you by guile [*dolos*]" (12:16). Through a series
of rhetorical questions (12:17–18), Paul denies that he took advantage of them and at the same time disavows that Titus, his
representative, presumed upon them. The Corinthians accuse Paul
of fraud, *dolos*, and Paul denies it. To the Thessalonians Paul
writes: "You know what kind of men we proved to be among you
for your sake" (1 Thess. 1:5). The Thessalonians even made Paul
their pattern (1:6). A few lines later he adds: "For our appeal
does not spring from error or uncleanness, nor is it made with
guile [*dolos*]; but just as we have been approved by God to be
entrusted with the gospel, so we speak, not to please men, but to
please God who tests our hearts" (2:3–4). Paul's appeal is made
in good faith, in response to God's commission. As long as God's
test of Paul's heart proves right Paul may rest assured that his
relationship to his "children," his fellow Christians, is as it should
be. When Paul proves to be the right person among the Thessalonians guile, *dolos*, is of course ruled out. "You are witnesses,

93

and God also, how holy and righteous and blameless was our behavior to you believers" (1 Thess. 2:10).

Sometime after Paul's era, Roman law reflects what must have
long since been a widespread uncertainty regarding how one is
to judge satisfactory performance of obligations in contracts. The
standard moves from what might be expected of some "ordinary
man" to one of the parties setting the norm by his own level of
performance.[31] Paul, in his preaching the gospel, his part of the
Jerusalem and Philippian *societates*, anticipates what only later
took place in Roman law and rigorously sets his own performance
as the norm by which all his partners (cf. Gal. 2:11 ff. and Phil.)
are to govern their care for the joint undertaking.[32]

As in the matters of *societas* already noted, this rigorous setting
of the norm filtered out into Paul's writing even to churches with
which *societas* was impossible or improbable. It became part of
Paul's means of conveying what is involved in living the gospel.
Imitatio Pauli communicates without the legal background or
framework, but that framework may help us estimate the importance of the motif of imitation.[33]

In this connection note the ways Paul certifies the quality of
the representatives sent in his absence. Matters such as their
trustworthiness and accomplishments are given, to be sure, but
Paul often comes down to the final certification: they behaved
among you as I did.[34] So the believers are to live their lives together by the standard established by Paul. *Imitatio Pauli* is informed by *societas Christi*.

SENTENTIAL REFLECTIONS OF *SOCIETAS*

In the material treated thus far, we have moved from the more
specific to the more general. We have seen that Paul understood
the Jerusalem conference to conclude in a *societas* and that Paul
and the Philippians understood themselves to be in a *societas* together. In this chapter we have seen that Paul addressed Philemon
as his partner (*socius*). Beyond that we have observed that cer-

94

tain aspects of *societas* made themselves visible across the Pauline correspondence.

There is now one final way in which *societas* may have made a broader impact on the Pauline correspondence, again not requiring the knowledge of the recipients for understanding. This has to do with another stage for the *societas* terminology or categories where they have become *sententiae* for Paul. Here our knowledge of their possible *societas* connection generally informs their possible meaning. In none of the following cases do we encounter an actual *societas*.

Occasionally Paul employs sententious epigrams in an effort to portray what is involved in living the Christian life with other Christians and in the world. Sometimes these epigrams, divorced from their original settings, are simply piled one upon the other. Such a case may be seen in the last half of Romans 12. In that context the *societas* terminology of *phronein* flashes in the midst of a string of vignettes of the Christian life properly lived. "Live in harmony with one another" (Rom. 12:16, *to auto eis allēlous phronountes*). Second Corinthians closes in similar form, with a series of sententious portraits of the life Paul wants them to lead, and once again the *societas* terminology is there at least for Paul and perhaps available to any reader who may know the wider context: "Mend your ways, heed my appeal, agree with one another [*to auto phroneite*], live in peace, and the God of love and peace will be with you" (2 Cor. 13:11). Once more in Romans, as Paul concludes his appeal to his readers, he resorts to the *societas* language: "May the God of steadfastness and encouragement grant you to live in such harmony [*to auto phronein*] with one another, in accord with Christ Jesus, that together you may with one voice glorify the God and Father of our Lord Jesus Christ" (15:5–6).

In the same epigrammatic materials noted above in Romans 12 when discussing the wider use of *phronein*, there is an appearance of *koinōnein* that could certainly be understood in a *societas* framework: "Contribute to the needs of the saints" (Rom. 12:13). The Greek for this phrase (*tais chreiais tōn hagiōn koinōnountes*) might be translated as sharing or partnering (*koinōnountes*) in the saints' needs. In Philippians *koinōnia* is the expression for *societas*. In Romans 12:13 it is not the specific realization of *societas* among Christians but appears in a more independent, sententious phrase to describe how the believers should care for one another. It has been dislodged from its original social matrix. Along the same lines but less epigrammatic and accordingly less general is the appearance of the verb and noun in Romans 15:25–27, a passage that we have seen to have connections for Paul at least with his Jerusalem *societas*. To be precise, however, the *societas* terminology here spills over beyond Paul's own carrying out of the contract proviso—remembering the poor—to portray how all Christians, Jews and Gentiles, relate to one another in Paul's delivery of the gift. Though it is Paul's keeping the commitment in good faith, he does not resist seeing the symbolism incorporating Jews and Gentiles. "At present, however, I am going to Jerusalem with aid for the saints. For Macedonia and Achaia have been pleased to make some contribution [*koinōnian tina poiēsasthai,* to do some *koinōnia/societas*] for the poor among the saints at Jerusalem" (Rom. 15:25–26). The *societas* terminology here soars. Paul uses it as a springboard for reflections concerning God's work in bringing the Jerusalem Christians and the Gentile Christians into partnership: the Gentiles become partners in the spiritual blessings of the Jewish Christians and thereby share the material blessings of the Gentiles with the poor among the saints at Jerusalem (Rom. 15:27).[35]

The *societas* terminology and categories functioned at several levels in Paul's letters: with a particular group of Christians, the Jerusalem pillars; with an entire congregation, the Philippians; with an individual among worshiping Christians, Philemon. Beyond this we can see that Paul has become so much at ease with the *societas* terminology and categories that he employs them without the requirement that the readers understand them as *societas* terms or understand themselves in *societas* with Paul. It is sometimes difficult, if not impossible, in the last phase to determine when for Paul the terminology retains an explicit connection to *societas*. Terminology that may have functioned specifically in *societas* settings has taken on a new, gnomic life that breaks out of its original social and legal context and assumes a fresh and independent life of its own in Pauline paraenesis.

NOTES

1. John Knox, *Philemon among the Letters of Paul*, rev. ed. (New York: Abingdon Press, 1959), maintains that the primary addressee of the letter is not Philemon but Archippus—and argues for a strong historical connection between this letter and Colossians on the basis of Col. 4:17. F. W. Beare, *St. Paul and His Letters* (New York: Abingdon Press, 1962), pp. 109–11, follows Knox both in seeing the letter addressed to Archippus and in stressing the letter's connection with Colossians.

2. Cf. Clinton W. Keyes, "The Greek Letter of Introduction," *AJP* 56 (1935): 28–44. More recently, William G. Doty, *Letters in Primitive Christianity* (Philadelphia: Fortress Press, 1973), reflects and assesses the current study of the Pauline letter forms, but letters of introduction or commendation are merely noted (cf. p. 16).

3. From 1874 to 1960 there are interpreters who fail to note the addressees other than Philemon, namely, Apphia, Archippus, and "the church in your house" (Phlem. 2). Contrast P. J. Gloag, *Introduction to the Pauline Epistles* (Edinburgh: T. & T. Clark, 1874), p. 303, and A. R. C. Leaney, *The Epistles to Timothy, Titus, and Philemon* (London: SCM Press, 1960), p. 135: The letter is not "addressed to an individual."

4. Jean Fleury, "Une Société de Fait dans l'Église Apostolique (Phil. 4:10 à 22)," in *Mélanges Philippe Meylan*, vol. 2, *Histoire du Droit* (Lausanne: Lausanne Université, 1963), p. 54, quotes Ulpian D. 17.2. 63: "*Hos enim summam rationem habet, cum societas ius quodammodo fraternitatis in se habet*" and then declares: "Cette remarque n'a rien d'étonnant étant connues les origines de la société de tous

biens, qui, dit Gaius, est *ad exemplum fratrum suorum*, à l'exemple des frères siens, le mot siens ayant le sense qu'il a dans l'expression héritiers siens, c'est-à-dire ceux qui se trouvent simultanément dans une même succession."

5. J. B. Lightfoot, *St. Paul's Epistles to the Colossians and to Philemon*, 9th ed. (London: Macmillan & Co., 1890), p. 342: "It is the entreaty of a brother to a brother on behalf of a brother." But the appeal that Philemon recognize Onesimus as brother is never simply based on Paul's evaluation of Onesimus as if "Paul hopes Philemon will share his regard for the returning slave." So John H. Schütz, *Paul and the Anatomy of Apostolic Authority* (Cambridge: Cambridge University Press, 1975), p. 222. Rather the decisive factor is that Onesimus is now to be reckoned a brother from two distinct perspectives: "both in the flesh and in the Lord" (Phlem. 16). So it is not just or even fundamentally Paul's regard for Onesimus that is critical; central instead is that Onesimus is now "in Christ"—as are Paul and Philemon.

6. Cf. Schütz, *Anatomy of Apostolic Authority*, p. 221: "In a curious little verse in Philemon [8], Paul parades a theoretical apostolic authority unmatched elsewhere in his letters." Schütz dubs it theoretical because Paul refuses to use it. I think it is not theoretical at all but given to Philemon as an alternate, back-up mode of Paul's relating to him. See n. 7 below.

7. There is a pattern in Paul of unexercised but claimed rights. The pattern deserves further study. In Philemon Paul has the right to command but does not use it. With the Corinthians he insists on his apostolic right to support but refuses to exercise it. In this connection cf. 1 Thess 2:6: "Nor did we seek glory from men, whether from you or from others, though we might have made demands as apostles of Christ."

8. Cf. C. J. Bjerkelund, *Parakalō* (Oslo: Universitetsforlaget, 1967), pp. 118–24, on Phlem. 8.

9. The terminology is stronger and more specific than Lightfoot's (*Epistles to the Colossians and to Philemon*, p. 341) translation—"thou holdest me to be a comrade, an intimate friend"—suggests. He takes a step in the right direction when after a reference to Phil. 2:29 he says: "Those are *koinōnoi*, who have common interests, common feelings, common work."

10. Cf. Hans Conzelmann, *1 Corinthians*, trans. James W. Leitch (Philadelphia: Fortress Press, 1975), p. 296. For a wide range of usage for *epistolē* see J. H. Moulton and G. Milligan, *The Vocabulary of the*

Further Reflections of *Societas* in the Pauline Correspondence

Greek New Testament, 2d ed. (London: Hodder and Stoughton, 1915), p. 246, and Henry G. Liddell and Robert Scott, eds., *Greek-English Lexicon,* 9th ed. (Oxford: Oxford University Press, 1940), p. 660.

11. To select or elect by raising hands. "Election or selection for definite offices or tasks." So F. Wilbur Gingrich and Frederick W. Danker, eds., *A Greek-English Lexicon of the New Testament,* 2d ed. rev. (Grand Rapids: Zondervan Publishing House, 1979), p. 881.

12. J. W. Jones, *The Law and Legal Theory of the Greeks* (Oxford: Clarendon Press, 1956), pp. 221–22: "The word *homologia,* from being the term for such a judicial admission of liability, came to mean any extra-judicial acknowledgement, whether of receipt of money, or of the authenticity of a written instrument, or of a seal and finally of any agreement. Admission and promise run into each other in the case of money obligations, so that it was a short step to the general use of the *homologia* for any promise of a future act, whether payment of money or not." In view of this consider the Corinthian commitment to the collection. As Paul concludes his remarks about it in 2 Corinthians 9, he refers to it as a "test of this service" (v. 13) and continues: "You will glorify God by your obedience *tēs homologias humōn eis to euaggelion tou Christou.*" In line with Jones's report on *homologia* this might appropriately be translated: "You will glorify God by your obedience in your promise regarding the gospel of Christ and by the generosity of your contribution [*koinōnias*] for them and for all others." In the context *homologia* fits in perfectly as "promise" or "commitment." For the *eis to euaggelion* here compare the *epi tē koinōnia humōn eis to euaggelion* of Phil. 1:5.

13. On the possibly limited enthusiasm of the Jerusalem poor on receipt of the collection see Ernst Haenchen, *The Acts of the Apostles* (Philadelphia: Westminster Press, 1971), pp. 613–14.

14. W. A. Beardslee, *Human Achievement and Divine Vocation in the Message of Paul* (Naperville: A. R. Allenson, 1961), p. 60: "It was his usual custom to work in a 'sweat-shop' trade and to carry on his missionary activity in his 'spare time.'" See Ronald F. Hock, "Paul's Working with His Hands" (diss., Yale University, 1975), for analogies in the Cynic tradition. Cf. also Hock's "Paul's Tentmaking and the Problem of His Social Class," *JBL* 97 (1978): 555–64.

15. 2 Thess. 3:6–13, though of questionable authenticity, makes a great deal out of Paul's toiling at a trade so that he can support himself and his preaching of the gospel. If 2 Thessalonians is not Pauline, then we have in it and certainly in Acts early portraits of Paul that

view him as regularly following this pattern of working and preaching. Little wonder that modern interpreters tend to follow the lead of those early Christian interpreters of Paul and enforce that view onto the authentic letters.

16. Walter Schmithals, *The Office of Apostle in the Early Church* (Nashville: Abingdon Press, 1969), p. 47: "This is a strange state of affairs. The apostle has the right to live off the gospel, because he is a preacher of it; at the same time, however, it is precisely the apostolic office itself which requires him to renounce his right in order not to give offense." The matter is not really so lofty and complicated as that. Paul simply does not get along with the Corinthians well enough for them not to misunderstand his taking support. From some Christians he can take assistance; from some he cannot. At stake is how much mutual trust is involved.

17. F. W. Beare, *A Commentary on the Epistle to the Philippians* (New York: Harper & Row, 1959), p. 152: "He always had the feeling that he was demeaning himself by accepting support; he was far happier when he could say: 'I will not be burdensome to you.'" This psychologizing interpretation simply does not square with the letters. On the contrary, when the conditions were right—as with the Philippians—Paul could and did take support. When the conditions were not right—as with the Corinthians—Paul did not and would not receive aid.

18. Cf. Robert W. Funk, "The Apostolic Parousia: Form and Significance," in *Christian History and Interpretation,* Studies Presented to John Knox, ed. W. R. Farmer, C. F. D. Moule, and R. R. Niebuhr (Cambridge: Cambridge University Press, 1967), pp. 249–68.

19. On the related issue of disappearance, cf. J. Zlinsky, "Zur Frage der Verschollenheit im römischen Recht," *AAASH* 8 (1960): 95–132.

20. C. H. Monro, ed. and trans., *Digest 17.2 Pro Socio* (Cambridge: Cambridge University Press, 1902), pp. 8–9.

21. Cf. Nils A. Dahl, "Paul and the Church at Corinth in 1 Cor. 1:10–4:21," in *Christian History and Interpretation,* esp. pp. 322–23.

22. Cf. 2 Cor. 2:9: "in order that I might know your *dokimē,* whether you are obedient in everything."

23. A possible second point of connection might be noted. In the opening verses of Philippians 2 we saw that to be "of one mind," to continue in *societas,* was equated paratactically with having "the same love" and being "in full accord" (*sumpsychoi*). The commendation of Timothy—"there is no one like Timothy" (*oudena gar echō isopsychon,* 2:20)—draws the attention back to the *societas* construc-

tion at the beginning of the chapter where the word *sumpsychoi* appeared.

24. By definition the "interests of Jesus Christ" are identical with the interests of those who are "in Christ."

25. A similar identification of Paul and Timothy occurs in 1 Cor. 16:10, where Paul advises the Corinthians—understandably without explicit *societas* connections—that Timothy should be put at ease when he comes, "for he is doing the work of the Lord, as I am."

26. See above, p. 13.

27. C. C. Turpin, "*Bonae Fidei Iudicia*," *CLJ* 23 (1965): 260–70. "*Fides* was a moral, originally a sacred principle, governing many relationships of Roman social life, such as those of patron and client, and tutor and pupil, and imposing obligations of true and faithful conduct. The obligations of *fides*, supported by religious sanction, were acknowledged also in the commerce between members of different communities. *Fides* required conformity with undertakings, and the view has much to support it that recourse was had to *fides* as an extralegal basis for the enforcement of relations not admitted by civil law, but in which a man had given his word. *Fides* required that his word must be kept, that his conduct should be in exact conformity with it. Thus was generated an obligation not unlike one arising from strict civil law" (p. 262). Further, p. 266: "*Fides* was appealed to as the foundation of the liability [in consensual contracts]; it was a familiar principle of moral and also of legal obligation."

28. Adolf Berger, *Encyclopedic Dictionary of Roman Law*, Transactions of the American Philosophical Society, N.S. 43, 2 (Philadelphia: American Philosophical Society, 1953), p. 471.

29. Francis de Zulueta, *The Institutes of Gaius*, pt. 2 (Oxford: Clarendon Press, 1953), p. 180.

30. Cf. Gaius 4. 182.

31. Today in American legal traditions the related and still functioning category is the "reasonable man." For a good general discussion of the complexity and flexibility of such a legal standard as reasonable man, see William L. Prosser, *Handbook of the Law of Torts* (St. Paul: West Publishing Co., 1964), pp. 153–68. And for an examination of the way the standard works with one class of legal problems, see Fleming James, "The Qualities of the Reasonable Man in Negligence Cases," *MLR* 16 (1951): 1–26.

32. I do not mean that this legal impetus to set the norm for satisfactory conduct in the performance of obligations is the only factor in Pauline imitation injunctions. In order to gain a full explanation of the

Pauline imitation phenomenon, one would no doubt have to reconstruct a combination of influences—one of which would be the strong
sense of obligation expressed and reinforced in Roman legal traditions.
Other influences would no doubt have to include the Cynic tradition
of the moral man, who out of his wish to "do good to men" sought "to
speak with *parrēsia* and to act as an example." For these and other
features of the Cynic tradition that may bear on Paul's imitation
theme, cf. Abraham J. Malherbe, " 'Gentle as a Nurse': The Cynic
Background to 1 Thess. 2," *NT* 12 (1970): 203–17. The words quoted
in this note are from 208.

33. On the imitation of Paul, see *TDNT*, s.v. *"mimeomai"*; D. M.
Stanley, " 'Become imitators of me': The Pauline Conception of Apostolic Tradition," *Bib* 40 (1959): 859–77; W. P. de Boer, *The Imitation of Paul* (Kampen: J. H. Kok, 1962); Anselm Schulz, *Nachfolgen
und Nachahmen, Studien zum Alten und Neuen Testament* 6 (Munich:
Kösel, 1962); and Hans Dieter Betz, "Nachfolge und Nachahmung
Jesu Christi im Neuen Testament," *BHTh* 37 (1967): 153–69.

34. Ramsey MacMullen, *Roman Social Relations, 50* B.C. *to* A.D.
284 (New Haven: Yale University Press, 1974), p. 65: "Romans preferred men's word to their property, their pledge to their deposit. The
cement of their daily financial relationships was people not things."

35. A similar use of *koinōnia* should be noted in 2 Cor. 8:4, again in
connection with the collection. Beyond that, I see no connection with
societas in the presence of *koinōnia* in the words of institution for the
Lord's Supper (1 Cor. 10:16) or in the opening words of the fragment
2 Cor. 6:14–7:1. The same goes for the surely traditional formulation
in Gal. 6:6.

6

Conclusions concerning *Societas* in the Pauline Corpus

The time has come to take inventory of what we have found. On the broadest scope, Paul used the Roman legal terminology and concepts of consensual *societas,* a well-established contract of partnership, in four distinct ways. First, Paul understood the Jerusalem conference (cf. Gal. 2:1–10) with Barnabas, James, John, and Cephas to have concluded in an actual *societas,* a partnership of equals, committed to the preaching of the one gospel to different audiences across the world known to them. When the Jerusalem pillars of the church saw God's grace at work in Paul and Barnabas, they gave to the latter the right hand of *societas.* Paul's faithful carrying out of the one contract requirement—that he remember the poor in Jerusalem—was understood by him not only to perform his contractual obligation to the pillars but, even more importantly, to present in symbolic fashion the whole Gentile mission of early Christianity to its spiritual forebears, Jewish Christianity. Acceptance of the offering by the representatives of the Jerusalem saints would complete the mission.

Second, in Philippians we saw that Paul had just received a payment or gift from the Philippians for at least the third time in their ongoing relationship. The last part of the canonical letter (4:10–20) is specifically prompted by the most recent gift-payment and is Paul's receipt. It is his reckoning of his account with the Philippians. Paul's proclamation of the gospel across the world

is his carrying out their mission as their representative. They therefore send support to him, and he accepts it. That the gift-payment from the Philippians to Paul was not just a token may be seen in several particulars: they have twice done it before, so there is a pattern of support; Paul had needed their support for some time before he received it in this last instance, but he quickly notes that they had not had an opportunity to give it to him (Phil. 4:10); and the language from the remainder of the letter shows that Paul understood himself to be in partnership (*societas*) with the Philippians "from the first day until now" (1:5). Paul's relation with the Philippians is singular, as he reminds them (4:15). With them alone of all his churches, Paul entered into the partnership so fully that he accepted their support. Only with the Philippians was the *societas Christi* so firmly established that he could use the language to conceptualize not only how he and the Christians ideally should relate to one another, but also how they might live the gospel to the fullest by supporting Paul when he was preaching as their representative. With no other church did he carry the *societas* relationship to that extreme.

There are at least two primary historical and sociological ingredients that engendered this special *societas* relation between Paul and the Philippians. One, the church was apparently little marked by internal strife; it was early and enduringly a stable, unified Christian community. Two, Philippi, because of its unusual status as a Roman colony, was proudly aware of the richness of Roman legal traditions. These ingredients were apparently catalyzed by Paul, himself a Roman citizen, and the outcome was the clearest case of a Christian community understanding itself as constituting with Paul a *societas Christi*.

The third distinct way in which the *societas* pattern and terminology have been seen to affect the Pauline corpus is in the Letter to Philemon. Here there is no indication that the *societas* concept has been taken as far as it was with the Philippians; no support has been sent to Paul. Rather the terminology of *societas* has been

directed to one person, Philemon, in the midst of a larger Christian community ("the church in your house"). Philemon has to decide whether he wants to continue in partnership with Paul. If he does, then he is to welcome back his runaway slave Onesimus as he would receive Paul himself, as Paul's double. How much the other recipients of the letter (Archippus and Apphia and "the church in your house") also understand themselves as Paul's partners is not clear. One of their number, Philemon, stands in the spotlight of a personal crisis centered upon the way he relates to the runaway slave, who has become his brother in Christ. Whether Paul and Philemon have entered into a formal *societas* cannot be answered unequivocally from the limited evidence provided by the letter. Nevertheless Paul casts Philemon's dilemma in *societas* terms: If you would remain in the partnership with me, receive him for what he is now, not what he was before. Now he is your brother in Christ—as I Paul am.

The fourth manner in which *societas* terminology manifests itself in Paul's correspondence is in epigrammatic, gnomic forms in which the language of *societas* has passed over from the particular contract situation to the more general, rhetorical one. Phrases such as *to auto phronein* (be "of the same mind") and terms such as *koinōnia* continue to function for Paul but do not require the recipients of those letters to understand them as contractual. For instance, *to auto phronein* occurs in the midst of a series of admonitions piled up by Paul at the end of canonical 2 Corinthians: "Finally, brethren, farewell. Mend your ways, heed my appeal, *agree with one another*, live in peace, and the God of love and peace will be with you" (13:11).

The Corinthians probably knew about consensual *societas* in their everyday business dealing—Corinth, like Philippi, was a Roman colony—but their Christian community was so strife-ridden that there was no chance for *societas Christi* to take root there. How could *societas Christi* function when Paul understands the Corinthians to accuse him of robbery and deceit (*dolos,* deceit, terminates *societas,* according to Roman law)?

Nevertheless for Paul *to auto phronein* in 2 Corinthians 13 may suggest the larger context of *societas,* but the Corinthians need not hold to that view of Christian community to see that Paul is calling for unity. At best the Corinthians are ready to understand *to auto phronein* on only the most minimal level of "living in peace" with one another. But for Paul the terminology seems to take on an independent life of its own, not requiring the full trappings of *societas Christi* for it to work in his communication with the Corinthians.

We have seen therefore that the terminology of *societas* functioned in the Pauline correspondence in a variety of ways. With most of his communities the requisite conditions of *societas*—harmony, good faith, and unity—were simply lacking, with the result that *societas Christi* could not be invoked as a way of conceptualizing Christian community. Where it could not, the language might continue to have a distinct life of its own but without the freight being carried by it in, say, Philippians or Philemon.

In Paul's letters *societas* is not some ethereal notion emptied of all its mundane, everyday connections. Specific, concrete transactions—an agreement concluding a historic meeting, a receipt for support, and the return of a runaway slave—have been the occasions when Paul reflected *societas* traditions. It is precisely in these day-to-day situations that *societas* is naturally at home. And Paul seizes these specific occasions as an opportunity to portray God's purposes for those whom he has called.

Societas is properly viewed as one among many images and ideas that Paul utilized to help Christians conceptualize their relation to one another and to their goals. Its range of usage appears limited precisely because the conditions necessary to its foundation—good faith and singleness of purpose—and fundamental to its continuation—unity and equality—were fragile and precarious to maintain. Where harmony, reciprocity, and equality prevailed, there *societas* could provide a framework in which Christians could relate to one another, to Paul, and to the preaching of the gospel beyond their borders.

106

Societas is in some respects a rather fragile contract, subject to dissolution on a variety of grounds, many of which are out of control of any one partner. Whereas one might abstain from fraud, one cannot necessarily prevent fraud on the part of another. Neither can one guarantee the dedication of another partner to the goals around which the partnership was established. Likewise one cannot enforce the reciprocity and equality so basic to *societas;* to do so would be a fundamental contradiction of *societas.* A failure at any of these points by any of the partners, and the *societas* crumbles. It is all the more remarkable that the *societas Christi* remained so effectively in force with the Philippian Christians and that Paul could risk Onesimus's well-being on his confidence that Philemon would choose to remain in partnership with Paul.

Societas is vulnerable on a number of counts, but it must also be observed that in some other respects *societas* provides a strong social bond. The different partners' commitment to a shared goal and their sense of brotherly equality can meld together into a strong sense of community. *Societas Christi* maximizes the sense of participation in the preaching mission. The Philippian Christians know themselves to be supporting Paul as their representative to preach the gospel. Their sense of participation in sharing the gospel with the rest of the world is no doubt heightened by their contributions to the support of Paul in his preaching mission.

At the same time, the Philippians *societas* shows evidence of a highly developed sense of the responsibility of the individual Philippian Christians to one another. Euodia and Syntyche are exhorted to be of the same mind, but that is no different from what is expected of all the Philippian believers, as is made clear in chapter 2. Most of all, however, *societas Christi* heightens individual self-determination. Philemon, for example, must determine for himself how he is going to relate to his partner in Christ, Paul. His own picture of himself in that relationship is his alone to develop. While *societas Christi* maximizes individual responsibility in the partnership, it minimizes social stratification

since social strata are not of consequence in *societas*. Persons of
very different social strata find themselves brought together in a
quasi-brotherly fashion. Philemon, slave owner, and Onesimus,
slave—even runaway slave—are brothers in Christ.

FURTHER IMPLICATIONS FOR OUR
UNDERSTANDING OF PAUL'S LETTERS

Let us turn now to some other implications of our study of
societas Christi for understanding problematical aspects of Paul's
letters. First, we confirm in new ways what others have suggested: the collection for Jerusalem assumes massive and in some
respects disproportionate importance in the Pauline corpus and
Paul's career as reflected by those letters. The Jerusalem conference, where the initial impetus for the collection occurs, comes
rather late in Paul's career; his churches are already established
and in operation.

It is possible to assess the significance of the collection on two
different levels, the one a strategic significance, the other a symbolic significance. The evidence in the four letters touching on
the collection suggests that much of Paul's energy at the end of
his career was spent in explaining how the gospel that he boasted
of preaching "free of charge" (1 Cor. 9:18) had all of a sudden
a price tag on it—or so some may have taken it. Not only that,
but the collection and its delivery ended Paul's career—another
index of its significance. In the face of known or suspected danger (Rom. 15:31), Paul determined to deliver the collection to
Jerusalem. Paul's extant writings do not give a further picture of
Paul's life or fate. If Acts is to be trusted here, Paul's fear of
trouble in Jerusalem in fact came to pass.

But Paul's determination to risk even his personal freedom—
and perhaps his life—by taking the collection to Jerusalem leads
us to the more important, namely, the symbolic, significance of
the collection. Paul's whole sense of his ministry, his entire career, hung in the balance around this collection. More than a

gift to alleviate suffering or hunger, the collection had come for Paul to symbolize the unity of the whole people of God produced by the preaching of the gospel. The one gospel preached to different groups—Jews and Gentiles alike—had produced one people of God.

A second implication of this study is that Paul's relationships with his different churches were not programmed for consistency and uniformity. On the face of it, it is evident that he got along differently with the diverse Christian communities that arose in response to his preaching. But beyond that it becomes clear that he adjusted himself and his circumstances to meet with the response that he received. With some of his churches, he worked on a self-support basis, never accepting any aid from them. Apparently at Corinth and Thessalonica he plied his own trade in order to support himself and preached to them as he had occasion. From the Corinthians he explicitly refused support, but while he was at Corinth he accepted assistance from the Philippian Christians. This was not a matter of duplicity on Paul's part. His relation with the Philippians enabled the acceptance of support from them. With the Corinthians he did not enjoy the trusting, good-faith relationship that would have made that possible. Paul's desire to be all things to all men (1 Cor. 9:19–23) worked itself out in very distinctive relationships with different Christian communities of believers. Accordingly, with some Christian communities, Paul established a special sense of *koinōnia*, while with others he was not able to do so.

A third implication of the study of *societas Christi* relates to the phrase *to auto phronein*, to be "of the same mind," especially as it occurs in Philippians 2. There the translation reads: "Have this mind among yourselves, which you have in Christ Jesus." We have seen that the fundamental phrase *to auto phronein* is reflective of *societas* contract terminology, relating to continued dedication to the original goal around which the contract was formed. It is accordingly not some mystical, inner-directed assimilation of the individual to the "mind of Christ." Rather Philippians 2 calls for the partners to retain their previous commitment to the partnership, which has Christ as its basis and focus.

Beyond the more specific implications of this study some by-products are generated. One is that the omnipresent problem of Paul's authority takes on a different cast in the contexts where *societas Christi* is functioning. Paul is never one to renounce his authority. He does not disclaim it. He goes out of his way with the Corinthians to insist upon his right as an apostle to receive support from his churches (1 Cor. 9:1–18) although with them he has chosen not to exercise that right. But he wants the record clear: the right is his; he simply eschews the enforcement of it. In a similar fashion we have seen that Paul does not doubt that he has the authority and insight to command an appropriate response from a believer such as Philemon who has come into the faith as a result of his preaching. But in the *societas* such a command—based on one's own personal authority over another person in the partnership—would be inappropriate, even alien. As in Corinthians, so in the *societas* context of Philemon, Paul affirms his authority to command faithful performance, but in Philemon, if the partnership is really working, Paul must forgo the use of command. The issue must be entrusted to the judgment of the partner. Because Paul was the father of Philemon's faith, he could command Philemon what to do with Onesimus, the runaway slave. But that option is explicitly rejected because it would be inappropriate. If Paul and Philemon are partners, have *societas* together, then one cannot command the other to performance. Each must allow the other the freedom to make his own judgments as to what action is appropriate to the *societas*. So Paul's authority is never out of the picture, but where *societas Christi* is in effect no command will be made on the basis of that apostolic authority. Paul is fully aware of that and "for love's sake" (v. 9) tells Philemon that if he is Paul's partner Philemon should receive Onesimus as Paul.

Another by-product of this investigation reflects on the Pauline understanding of freedom. As he declares to the Corinthians, he preaches the gospel out of necessity not freedom of will (1 Cor. 9:16). But that obligation does not rule out his freedom willingly and even joyfully to do what is required. In similar fashion the responsibility to remember the poor in Jerusalem was assumed by Paul as a contractual obligation to the Jerusalem pillars, but it was something he was eager to do. For Paul, one can freely take up one's obligations; Christian freedom makes that possible. In Paul's view obligation does not rule out freedom.

Other features of the Pauline correspondence may have been informed or influenced by Paul's appropriation of *societas* as a means of understanding Christian community. Chief among those might be the sense in which Paul, by his own care concerning his obligations, sets the norms for other Christians in their commitments. Paul's enjoinders to imitate him do not cover all aspects of his life. Christians are not to be like Paul in every particular. Rather they are to comport themselves in the community as he does. We have seen that Paul views himself as setting the standard of conduct appropriate to the *societas Christi*: seeking the interests of others above his own, carrying his own part of the burden, and so forth.

Societas may also have shed some light on the care Paul takes in certifying the high caliber of his representatives. A *societas* partner absent against his will, as Paul frequently declares himself to be, might be absolved from partnership responsibilities. Clearly, Paul does not want to be relieved of those commitments. Roman legal tradition allows for certified representatives to carry on the endeavors of the partnership. Timothy and Titus are described in such a way as to become Paul's doubles, carrying on his work with the various Christian churches.

THE LIMITS OF *SOCIETAS* IN PAUL'S FORMULATIONS

It might be helpful at this juncture to declare what we did *not* find in this study. First, *societas Christi* is not an all-pervasive model of the Christian community. As we have seen, its flowering requires certain very specific conditions—and those conditions were infrequently reflected in the Pauline correspondence. Much as the "body of Christ" model was invoked by Paul in a certain limited range of circumstances, so *societas Christi* functioned for Paul when the circumstances allowed it.[1]

Tied up with this first observation is a second. *Societas* is used by Paul with isolable groups: the Jerusalem pillars, the Philippian believers, and Philemon. The *societas* partnership does not provide any overarching structure that links the various Christian communities together. As "church" in the unquestionably authentic Pauline letters seems regularly to be very localized—"the church in your house"—so *societas Christi* seems to be also. Never once does Paul write to persons who might contribute to the collection that they can thereby become partners with the Jerusalem pillars as he and Barnabas are. Not a single time does Paul indicate to anyone at Philippi that their partnership includes Christians other than themselves and Paul. One might suggest that he comes the closest to such a claim when he recognizes that the Gentiles are indebted to the Jerusalem, Jewish Christians and suggests a reciprocity that is not alien to *societas*. "For Macedonia and Achaia have been pleased to make some contribution [do some *koinōnia*] for the poor among the saints at Jerusalem; they were pleased to do it, and indeed they are in debt to them, for if the Gentiles have come to share in their spiritual blessings, they ought also to be of service to them in material blessings" (Rom. 15:26–27). Apart from that we have no clue that *societas Christi* ever functioned in the overarching fashion that, say, "church" does in Ephesians.[2]

Third, Paul never includes Christ or God as partner or partners in the *societas*. The *societas* always is in service of Christ or God but never includes either of them as a part of it. Neither are the believers partners with Christ or with God. Christians remain partners with each other, given to one another in Christ.

No matter how much Paul may have co-opted *societas* as a way

of expressing the nature and purpose of Christian life, he did not
do it in a rigid way. At several points he has heightened certain
features of *societas* in an effort to highlight what he deemed important. For example, only with the Philippians did Paul carry
societas to its full expression of support for work undertaken in
behalf of the partnership. When addressing Philemon the stress
falls much more heavily on the brotherly character of the partnership. And, finally, when describing the Jerusalem *societas*, Paul
accents the equality of the partners as a way of controverting a
Galatian notion that Paul was subordinate to the Jerusalem pillars. In each manifestation of the *societas* conceptualization different aspects of *societas* have been stressed as the occasion or situation warranted. Paul's employment of *societas* is therefore pre-
dictably flexible. What he accents about *societas* indicates his
apprehension of the situation he faces with a given group of
Christians.

But Paul not only is creatively flexible in stressing certain features of *societas* as the situation may demand, he also takes some
liberties with the legal traditions concerning *societas*. At least
two prominent examples may be cited. First, Paul introduces to
societas a notion nowhere found in the legal traditions and
papyri: the idea of a surrogate partner introduced into an already
established *societas*. Paul and Philemon are the partners. Paul
indicates to Philemon that he must decide whether he continues
to have partnership with Paul. If he does, he is to receive
Onesimus "as me" (*hōs eme*). Onesimus, the runaway slave,
stands in for Paul. He is now, like Paul, a brother in Christ to
Philemon. It is as if a new partner is introduced into the already
established partnership. Roman law has no provision for that; a
new partnership would have to be established. But Paul's creative
appropriation of *societas* allows him to alter it for his own purposes in view of his understanding of Christian community.

There is a second major way in which Paul departs from the
standard legal understanding of *societas*. According to Roman
law consensual *societas* terminates when the consensus is lost,

when the partners are no longer of one mind. If there is dissension or difference of opinion, *societas* is in danger. We do not have enough information to know whether Paul ever used the *societas* model with a Christian community only to have it fractured by dissension. But we do know that Paul never simply used *societas* alone as a way of understanding how Christians ought to relate to one another and to the world outside. Whenever *societas* is employed by Paul, it always appears in conjunction with other models of Christian community. We can see in the Letter to Philemon that although the *societas* relationship is preferred by Paul in this instance, his apostolic authority is flashed as a backup to insure that the community continues, that love is performed, that the good is accomplished. According to strict legal tradition *societas* racked by dissension terminates. Christian community begun as *societas* can continue in other ways should dissension obviate that way of understanding Christian community. Paul can relate to his fellow Christians as the one to whom they owe their very selves (Phlem. 19) or as a father to his children (1 Cor. 4:14–15)—or any of several other modes—if the relationship of equal partners becomes inoperative. Under Roman law, if *societas* crumbles, the former partners simply go their separate ways. With Paul's use of *societas*, if full equality among the partners fails, other modes of relationship among Christians come into operation. In the case of Philemon, for example, if Philemon's own free will did not engender love for Onesimus, Paul can fall back upon command, though Paul prefers not to do so if there is an alternative.

PAUL'S VIEW OF CHRISTIANS IN THE WORLD

Finally, this study shows that Paul creatively took over a contract that functioned widely in transactions of his day and saw ways of expressing what he knew to be possible for believers in Christ. His usage did not pull those people out of the social and legal matrix in which they lived before their call; rather it took a social covenant from that context and applied it to the prac-

114

tical situation of believers who formerly did not belong to one another as they sought ways to express their faith and their new situation in Christ. In the contexts where it was viable, what people understood from their own social and legal backgrounds now served them as they tried to understand the parameters of their new life in Christ.

Societas Christi shows up most clearly in the Pauline writings exactly at those points where transactions are taking place, in very earthy situations—where a consensus is reached, where a payment-gift has been received by Paul, and where a runaway slave is being returned. It is these mundane, this-worldly situations that are the occasion for Paul to use the *societas* terminology. *Societas Christi* was not an escape from the world—neither on some inner-directed, mystical solo journey nor on some collective flight away to a "safe" place. Rather *societas Christi* not only provided a social framework in which Christians could understand and creatively fulfill their mutual obligations within the community; it also became the means by which Christians could accomplish their common mission to share the gospel with the rest of the world.

NOTES

1. Robert Jewett, *Paul's Anthropological Terms* (Leiden: E. J. Brill, 1971), pp. 248–50.
2. Cf. my treatment of the authorship problem regarding Ephesians and my comments on the view of the church there: "The Letter to the Ephesians," in *Ephesians, Colossians, 2 Thessalonians, The Pastoral Epistles,* ed. Gerhard Krodel (Philadelphia: Fortress Press, 1978).

Selected Bibliography

(Works Mentioned in This Text)

Allan, J. A. *The Epistle of Paul the Apostle to the Galatians*. London: SCM Press, 1954.

Ball, W. E. B. *St. Paul and the Roman Law*. Edinburgh: T. & T. Clark, 1901.

Bardy, Gustave. "Saint Paul Juriste." *RechScRel* 31 (1943): 209–10.

Barrow, R. H. *Slavery in the Roman Empire*. London: Methuen and Co., 1928.

Bartsch, H. W. "... wenn ich ihnen dies Frucht versiegelt habe. Röm. 15:28. Ein Beitrag zum Verständnis der paulinischen Mission." *ZNW* 63 (1972): 95–107.

Beardslee, W. A. *Human Achievement and Divine Vocation in the Message of Paul*. Naperville: A. R. Allenson, 1961.

Beare, F. W. *A Commentary on the Epistle to the Philippians*. New York: Harper & Row, 1959.

———. *St. Paul and His Letters*. New York: Abingdon Press, 1962.

Berger, Adolf. *Encyclopedic Dictionary of Roman Law*. Transactions of the American Philosophical Society, N. S. 43, 2. Philadelphia: American Philosophical Society, 1953.

Betz, Hans Dieter. "Nachfolge und Nachahmung Jesu Christi im Neuen Testament." *BHTh* 37 (1967): 153–69.

Bjerkelund, C. J. *Parakalô*. Oslo: Universitetsforlaget, 1967.

Bolkestein, H. *Wohltätigkeit und Armenpflege im vorchristlichen Altertum*. Utrecht: A. Oosthoek, 1939.

Boucaud, Charles. "Saint Paul Jurisconsulte." *QI* (Avril 1940): 83.

Brandt, W. *Dienst und Dienen im Neuen Testament*. Gütersloh: C. Bertelsmann, 1931.

Bring, Ragnar. *Commentary on Galatians*. Translated by E. Wahlstrom. Philadelphia: Muhlenberg Press, 1961.

Bruce, F. F. *1 and 2 Corinthians*. London: Oliphants, 1971.

Buckland, W. W. *The Roman Law of Slavery*. Cambridge: Cambridge University Press, 1908.

———. *A Text-book of Roman Law from Augustus to Justinian*. Cambridge: Cambridge University Press, 1921.

Burton, E. D. *Critical and Exegetical Commentary on the Epistle to the Galatians*. New York: Charles Scribner's Sons, 1920.

Campbell, J. Y. "KOINŌNIA and its Cognates in the New Testament." *JBL* 51 (1932): 352–80.

Cerfaux, Lucien. *Le Chrétien dans la Théologie Paulinienne*. Paris: Editions du Cerf, 1962.

Cohen, Boaz. *Jewish and Roman Law: A Comparative Study*. New York: Jewish Theological Seminary of America, 1966.

Collart, Paul. *Philippes Ville de Macédoine*. Paris: E. de Boccard, 1937.

Conrat, Max. "Das Erbrecht im Galaterbrief (3,15–4,7)." *ZNW* 5 (1904): 204–27.

Conzelmann, Hans. *1 Corinthians*. Translated by James W. Leitch. Philadelphia: Fortress Press, 1975.

Crook, John. *Law and Life of Rome*. Ithaca: Cornell University Press, 1967.

Dahl, Nils A. "Paul and the Church at Corinth in 1 Cor. 1:10–4:21." In *Christian History and Interpretation*. Studies Presented to John Knox, edited by W. R. Farmer, C. F. D. Moule, and R. R. Niebuhr. Cambridge: Cambridge University Press, 1967.

Danker, F. W. "Under Contract: A Form-Critical Study of Linguistic Adaptation in Romans." In *Festschrift to Honor F. Wilbur Gingrich*, edited by E. H. Barth and R. E. Cocroft, pp. 91–114. Leiden: E. J. Brill, 1972.

Daube, David. "*Societas* as a Consensual Contract." *CLJ* 6 (1938): 381–403.

de Boer, W. P. *The Imitation of Paul*. Kampen: J. H. Kok, 1962.

Deissmann, Adolf. *Bible Studies*. Translated by A. Grieve. Edinburgh: T. & T. Clark, 1909.

———. *Light from the Ancient East*. 4th ed. Translated by L. R. M. Strachan. New York: George H. Doran Co., 1927.

Delcor, Mathias. "The Courts of the Church of Corinth and the Courts of Qumran." In *Paul and Qumran: Studies in New Testament Exegesis*, edited by J. Murphy-O'Connor, pp. 69–84. London: G. Chapman, 1968.

Selected Bibliography

Delling, Gerhard. "Ehescheidung." *RAC* 4: 707–19.

Dinkler, Erich. "Zum Problem der Ethik bei Paulus: Rechtsnahme und Rechtsverzicht (1 Kor 6:1–11)." *ZTK* 49 (1952): 167–200.

Dodd, C. H. "The Mind of Paul: I." In *New Testament Studies*. New York: Charles Scribner's Sons, n.d.

Doty, William G. *Letters in Primitive Christianity*. Philadelphia: Fortress Press, 1973.

Eger, Otto. "Rechtsworte und Rechtsbilder in den paulischen Briefen." *ZNW* 18 (1917): 84–108.

Ellicott, C. J. *A Critical and Grammatical Commentary on St. Paul's Epistles to the Philippians, Colossians, and to Philemon*. Boston: Draper and Halliday, 1866.

Finley, M. I., ed. *Slavery in Classical Antiquity*. New York: Barnes & Noble, 1968.

Fleury, Jean. "Une Société de Fait dans l'Église Apostolique (Phil. 4:10 à 22)." In *Mélanges Philippe Meylan*. Vol. 2. *Histoire du Droit* (Lausanne: Lausanne Université, 1963), pp. 41–59.

Funk, Robert W. "The Apostolic Parousia: Form and Significance." In *Christian History and Interpretation*. Studies Presented to John Knox, edited by W. R. Farmer, C. F. D. Moule, and R. R. Niebuhr, pp. 249–68. Cambridge: Cambridge University Press, 1967.

Furnish, Victor P. *Theology and Ethics in Paul*. Nashville: Abingdon Press, 1968.

Gager, John G. *Kingdom and Community: The Social World of Early Christianity*. Englewood Cliffs, N.J.: Prentice Hall, 1975.

Garnsey, Peter. *Social Status and Legal Privilege in the Roman Empire*. Oxford: Clarendon Press, 1970.

Gloag, P. J. *Introduction to the Pauline Epistles*. Edinburgh: T. & T. Clark, 1874.

Grayston, K. "The Significance of the Word *Hand* in the New Testament." In *Mélanges Biblique en hommage au R. P. Béda Rigaux*. Gembloux: Duculot, 1970.

Greenidge, A. H. J. *Infamia: Its Place in Roman Public and Private Law*. Oxford: Clarendon Press, 1894.

Haenchen, Ernst. *The Acts of the Apostles*. Translated by B. Noble and G. Shinn. Philadelphia: Westminster Press, 1971.

Hall, D. R. "St. Paul and Famine Relief: A Study in Galatians 2:10." *ExpT* 82 (1971): 309–11.

Hengel, Martin. *Property and Riches in the Early Church*. Translated by J. Bowden. Philadelphia: Fortress Press, 1974.

Hock, Ronald F. "Paul's Tentmaking and the Problem of His Social Class." *JBL* 97 (1978): 555–64.

———. "Paul's Working with His Hands." Dissertation, Yale University, 1975.

Hofius, O. *Der Christushymnus Phil 2, 6–11*. Untersuchungen zur Gestalt und Aussage eines urchristlichen Psalms. Tübingen: J. C. B. Mohr (Paul Siebeck), 1976.

Holl, K. "Der Kirchenbegriff des Paulus in seinem Verhältnis zu dem der Urgemeinde." In *Gesammelte Aufsätze*. Tübingen: J. C. B. Mohr, 1928.

Horowitz, George. *The Spirit of Jewish Law*. New York: Central Book Co., 1953.

Huwardas, Stawros G. *Beiträge zum griechischen und gräkoägyptischen Eherecht der Ptolemäer- und frühen Kaiserzeit*. Leipzig: T. Weicher, 1931.

James, Flemming. "The Qualities of the Reasonable Man in Negligence Cases." *MLR* 16 (1951): 1–26.

Jewett, Robert. *Paul's Anthropological Terms*. Leiden: E. J. Brill, 1971.

Jolowicz, H. F. *Historical Introduction to the Study of Roman Law*. Cambridge: Cambridge University Press, 1965.

Jones, A. H. M. "Slavery in the Ancient World." *EHR* 9 (1956): 185–99.

Jones, J. W. *The Law and Legal Theory of the Greeks*. Oxford: Clarendon Press, 1956.

Juster, Jean. *Les Juifs dans l'Empire romain*. Paris: P. Geuthner, 1914.

Käsemann, Ernst. *Perspectives on Paul*. Translated by M. Kohl. Philadelphia: Fortress Press, 1969.

Keck, L. E. "The Poor among the Saints in the New Testament." *ZNW* 56 (1965): 100–129.

Keyes, Clinton W. "The Greek Letter of Introduction." *AJP* 56 (1935): 28–44.

Knox, John. *Chapters in a Life of Paul*. New York: Abingdon-Cokesbury Press, 1950.

———. *Philemon among the Letters of Paul*. Rev. ed. New York: Abingdon Press, 1959.

Lagrange, M.-J. *Saint Paul Épitre aux Galates*. Paris: Gabalda, 1942.

Leaney, A. R. C. *The Epistles to Timothy, Titus, and Philemon*. London: SCM Press, 1960.

Lemerle, Paul. *Philippes et la Macédoine Orientale*. Paris: E. de Boccard, 1945.

Selected Bibliography

Liebenam, Wilhelm. *Zur Geschichte und Organisation des romisches Vereinswesens.* Leipzig: B. G. Teubner, 1890.

Lightfoot, J. B. *St. Paul's Epistles to the Colossians and to Philemon.* London: Macmillan & Co., 1890.

————. *St. Paul's Epistle to the Galatians.* 2d ed. London: Macmillan & Co., 1866.

————. *St. Paul's Epistle to the Philippians.* London: Macmillan & Co., 1869.

Longenecker, R. N. *Paul, Apostle of Liberty.* Grand Rapids: Eerdmans, 1964.

Lyall, F. "Roman Law in the Writings of Paul. Adoption." *JBL* 88 (1969): 458–66.

————. "Roman Law in the Writings of Paul. The Slave and the Freedman." *NTS* 17 (1970): 73–79.

MacMullen, Ramsey. *Roman Social Relations, 50 B.C. to A.D. 284.* New Haven: Yale University Press, 1974.

Malherbe, Abraham J. " 'Gentle as a Nurse': The Cynic Background to 1 Thess 2." *NT* 12 (1970): 203–17.

————. *Social Aspects of Early Christianity.* Baton Rouge: Louisiana State University Press, 1977.

Martin, R. P. *Carmen Christi: Philippians 2:5–11 in Recent Interpretation and in the Setting of Early Christian Worship.* Cambridge: Cambridge University Press, 1967.

Meeks, Wayne A. "The Social World of Early Christianity." *BullCSR* 6 (1975): 1.

————, ed. *The Writings of St. Paul.* New York: W. W. Norton & Co., 1972.

Minear, Paul S. *The Obedience of Faith.* London: SCM Press, 1971.

Monro, C. H., ed. and trans. *Digest 17. 2 Pro Socio.* Cambridge: Cambridge University Press, 1902.

Moule, C. F. D. "Further Reflections on Philippians 2:5–11." In *Apostolic History and the Gospel: Biblical and Historical Essays presented to F. F. Bruce,* edited by W. W. Gasque and R. P. Martin. Grand Rapids: Eerdmans, 1970.

Munck, Johannes. *Paul and the Salvation of Mankind.* Translated by F. Clarke. Richmond: John Knox Press, 1959.

Nicholas, Barry. *An Introduction to Roman Law.* Oxford: Clarendon Press, 1962.

Nickle, Keith F. *The Collection: A Study in Paul's Strategy.* Naperville: A. R. Allenson, 1966.

Pfitzner, Victor C. *Paul and the Agon Motif.* Leiden: E. J. Brill, 1967.

Poland, Franz. *Geschichte des griechischen Vereinswesens.* Leipzig: B. G. Teubner, 1909.

Ramsay, W. M. *A Historical Commentary on St. Paul's Epistle to the Galatians.* New York: G. P. Putnam's Sons, 1900.

Ridderbos, H. N. *The Epistle of Paul to the Churches of Galatia.* Grand Rapids: Eerdmans, 1953.

Rist, John M. *Stoic Philosophy.* London: Cambridge University Press, 1969.

Robinson, A. W. *The Epistle of Paul the Apostle to the Galatians.* London: Methuen, 1900.

Sampley, J. Paul. " 'Before God, I do not lie' (Gal. 1:20): Paul's Self-Defence in the Light of Roman Legal Praxis." *NTS* 23 (1977): 477–82.

————. "The Letter to the Ephesians." In *Ephesians, Colossians, 2 Thessalonians, The Pastoral Epistles,* edited by Gerhard Krodel. Philadelphia: Fortress Press, 1978.

————. "*Societas Christi:* Roman Law and Paul's Conception of the Christian Community." In *God's Christ and His People.* Festschrift in honor of Nils A. Dahl, edited by W. A. Meeks and J. Jervell, pp. 158–74. Oslo: University of Oslo Press, 1977.

Sass, S. L. "Research in Roman Law: Guide to Sources." *LLJ* 56 (1963): 210–33.

Schmithals, Walter. *The Office of Apostle in the Early Church.* Translated by J. E. Steely. Nashville: Abingdon Press, 1969.

————. *Paul and James.* Translated by C. M. Barton. London: SCM Press, 1965.

Schoeps, H. J. *Paul: The Theology of the Apostle in Light of Jewish Religious History.* Philadelphia: Westminster Press, 1961.

Schulz, Anselm. *Nachfolgen und Nachahmen, Studien zum Alten und Neuen Testament* 6 (Munich: Kösel, 1962).

Schütz, John H. *Paul and the Anatomy of Apostolic Authority.* Cambridge: Cambridge University Press, 1975.

Sevenster, J. N. *Paul and Seneca.* Leiden: E. J. Brill, 1961.

Shagli, Moshe. "Aristotle's Concept of Responsibility and its Reflection in Roman Jurisprudence." *ILR* 6 (1971): 39–64.

Smith, Jonathan Z. "The Social Description of Early Christianity." *RSR* 1 (1975): 19–21.

Stanley, D. M. " 'Become imitators of me': The Pauline Conception of Apostolic Tradition." *Bib* 40 (1959): 859–77.

Selected Bibliography

Strecker, G. "Redaktion und Tradition im Christus-Hymnus Phil. 2." *ZNW* 55 (1964): 63–78.

Stuhlmacher, P. *Das paulinische Evangelium. I. Vorgeschichte.* Göttingen: Vandenhoeck & Ruprecht, 1968.

Szlechter, Emile. *Le Contrat de Société en Babylonie, en Grèce, et à Rome.* Paris: Recueil Sirey, 1947.

Taylor, Greer M. "The Function of *PISTIS CHRISTOU* in Galatians." *JBL* 85 (1966): 58–76.

Turpin, C. C. "*Bonae Fidei Iudicia.*" *CLJ* 24 (1965): 260–70.

Usteri, L. *Commentar über den Brief pauli an die Galater.* Zürich: Orell Füssli, 1833.

Waltzing, J. -P. *Etude historique sur les corporations professionelles chez les Romains.* 4 vols. Brussels: F. Hayez, 1895–96.

Watson, Alan. "Consensual *Societas* between Romans and the Introduction of Formulae." *RIDA* 9 (1962): 431–36.

———. "Illogicality and Roman Law." *ILR* 7 (1972): 14–24.

———. *The Law of Obligations in the Later Roman Republic.* Oxford: Clarendon Press, 1965.

———. *The Law of the Ancient Romans.* Dallas: Southern Methodist University Press, 1970.

Wegner, Michael. *Untersuchungen zu der lateinischen Begriffen socius und societas.* Göttingen: Vandenhoeck & Ruprecht, 1969.

Wilken, Robert L. "Toward a Social Interpretation of Early Christian Apologetics." *CH* 39 (1970): 437–58.

Williams, Arthur Lukyn. *The Epistle of Paul the Apostle to the Galatians.* Cambridge: Cambridge University Press, 1936.

Wilson, S. G. *The Gentiles and the Gentile Mission in Luke-Acts.* Cambridge: Cambridge University Press, 1973.

Zlinsky, J. "Zur Frage der Verschollenheit im römischen Recht." *AAASH* 8 (1960): 95–132.

Zulueta, Francis de. *The Institutes of Gaius.* Pt. 1, Text. Pt. 2, Commentary. Oxford: Clarendon Press, 1953.

Index of Cited Biblical Passages

Index of Cited Biblical Passages

Index of Cited Biblical Passages

An aspect of Roman contractual law provided the framework for understanding several of Paul's seminal theological ideas — ie Koinonia, partnership in Gospel, why he accepted money of Philippi but not Corinth. Concept is called consensual societas — a legal instrument for formalizing an agreement between 2 or more persons based on a common aim, trust, mutual obligation, — ie "unity".

Thus the Jeru Conf. was seen as such — w/ Paul oblig to the contract to reach Gentiles — & to bring a collection to Jeru poor. The Philip. relationship was based heavily on the idea & & Philemon.

↓
etc.

for review — see ch(
& last chap

flim flam

X 9, (3) on Jas 2:6
88 'y ford with' Jas 4-5

The best
I've seen

X Ch 4 on Philippians 4:10-20
87f 84f 106 103f
109

? my sermon
on Ch 4

79f on Philemon 113 104
10

85 I Cor — on free NOT
105 to eat meat

95 on Rom 12:3f

113 Gal.